MW00984600

EATING ON THE

Run

Survival Foraging for Plants, Grasses, Nuts, and Berries

FRED DEMARA

PALADIN PRESS • BOULDER, COLORADO

Eating on the Run:
Survival Foraging for Plants, Grasses, Nuts, and Berries
by Fred Demara

Copyright © 2012 by Fred Demara

ISBN 13: 978-1-61004-763-0
Printed in the United States of America

Published by Paladin Press, a division of
Paladin Enterprises, Inc.
Gunbarrel Tech Center
7077 Winchester Circle
Boulder, Colorado 80301 USA, +1.303.443.7250

Direct inquiries and/or orders to the above address.

PALADIN, PALADIN PRESS, and the "horse head" design
are trademarks belonging to Paladin Enterprises and
registered in United States Patent and Trademark Office.

Front cover photos—Row 1 (left to right): University of Arizona, Tucson, Boyce
Thompson Arboretum; iStockphoto.com/merrymoonmary. Row 2: Author. Row 3:
Author. Row 4: University of Arizona, Tucson, Boyce Thompson Arboretum;
iStockphoto.com/Andrew Kravchenko.

Back cover photos (left to right)—Author; Author; University of Arizona, Tucson,
Boyce Thompson Arboretum; Author

Neither the author nor the publisher assumes
any responsibility for the use or misuse of
information contained in this book.

Visit our website at www.paladin-press.com

CONTENTS

PREFACE

There are some 2,000 edible and nutritious plants recorded. Most are not cultivated as a crop. Growing wild, these little-appreciated but healthful and palatable plants can feed you well when you are on your own in the wilderness. They hold the potential to provide something wholesome to eat at every time of year, in virtually every venue. I have selected the most universal candidates of North America for this volume.

You only need to know which of these plants are the best food and the easiest to find in order to fuel your travel and survival as you return to, or get to, your home base. The hope is that this book will equip the reader with a working knowledge of worthwhile, proven, and readily harvested food sources common to the North American wilderness. They sustained earlier cultures for thousands of years, and they could save your life today.

INTRODUCTION
Let's Eat!

"Ewww, eating weeds and grass," you say? How about lobster, crabs, crayfish, corn, rice, and wheat? They're all weeds and grass . . .

If you are in a "survival" situation in the wilderness, and hungry, you may have to follow Teddy Roosevelt's advice and "do the best you can, with what you have, where you are." The good news is that the odds are in your favor, that the food you need will be "where you are," if you know which ones will serve your purpose. This book has been written to show you a broad selection of commonly encountered plants, at least some of which are likely to be found any time of year across North America, which can provide you the body fuel to get home or to get away, as may be your immediate need.

Although definitions vary, nibbling around the edges of a mountain of freeze-dried chow in a warm cabin really isn't "surviving"— that's living high on the hog. Being cold, wet, hungry, alone, and eating what's there, because you know what's good, is our working definition here. And "what's there" can be really good. And in any case, what's all this talk about going into the woods and "surviving"? The American natives that the Europeans found, and the aboriginal peoples who preceded them (such as the Walla Walla Man, Clovis Man, and probably others) did not "survive" in the North American wilderness: they simply *lived* here, thank you very much. You can too. One of their crucial skill sets would have been to learn just what was growing around them that was good to eat. We can, too, and the generations that have gone before have saved us a lot of trial and error.

One can hypothesize who these first North American people

were, where they came from, and how they got here. But one conclusion is obvious on its own face: whencesoever they came, one of the first things they had to figure out was, *hey, what's for dinner?* Any first arrivals would have had to live as nomadic hunter-gatherers, although it apparently did not take long for the advanced civilizations on the East Coast to become engaged in sophisticated farming of corn (maize), various beans, squashes, grains, and potherbs. But these crops were not their only staples.

A lot of their everyday diet was never farmed, because they did not have to, any more than they had to farm fish and raise venison. Nature was the farmer, and the hungry were the harvesters, Garden of Eden style. At the same time that some aboriginal peoples in the Americas raised corn, squash, and beans, there were also primarily nomadic people who followed suitable vegetation and animals. As long as the population pressure didn't exceed nature's bounty, they did fine. Almost everybody likes to be omnivorous, but in reality, either in a nomadic or survival scenario, the wild vegetables that you have beat the venison roast you do not, or the tasty cottontail you cannot take the time to cook if you have to keep moving.

Until settlements were established and crops developed and planted, with the tools one can assume or find evidence they had, it's a safe bet that hunting-gathering entailed a lot more successful gathering of plants. Although then, as now, hunting big game and fishing salmon might be more fun. Simply put, plants are a lot easier to catch barehanded.

Probably within a surviving generation, new arrivals would have sorted out which plants were good to eat, which ones made you sick, which ones would kill you, and which ones could either be used as medicine or would bite back. They would have learned where to find and harvest them, as well as how to prepare, preserve, and enjoy them.

European settlers quickly learned from the natives about plants they were not familiar with in Europe, and many wild plants native here or brought from Europe are still staples in rural American diets today.

Nutritionally, some of the veggies are a quantum leap ahead of what's available in a modern supermarket, and the reason we find a vegetable in stores usually has more to do with its amenability to mechanical harvest and efficient shipping/storage than its tastiness and nutritional value. It's worth bearing in mind that what decides whether a plant becomes a commercial "crop" has primarily to do with its profitability. Profitability is a combination of factors such as cost of growing, merchantability (appearance and taste), how well it ships and displays before it degrades, what its storage life is, and often, almost as an afterthought, sometimes its nutritional value. Nature's wild vegetable bounty is largely ignored, except for a few notables such as purslane, now found in yuppie restaurants; some seasonal potherbs, greens, and wild fruits; and a few wild nuts and seeds.

A "weed," after all, is merely a plant growing where you don't want it, and many of the weeds that abound in wholesome environs—such as wilderness, fencerows, fields, and even your own veggie patch—are fair game. Learn how to cast a broader net as you glean "where you are," because these Rodney Dangerfields of the plant world are worth a closer look. Many are tastier than those you can buy, often more nutritious, and free. And these good options for survival chow are all over—with a little luck, right where and when you need them.

Additionally, having grown unmolested for generations, these wild crops can offer some pretty easy picking any time of year, and they are are available even if you have to keep moving to get where you are going. There is something to eat just about every place any-body has ever lived in North America. The old-timers had to eat, too, you know, so let's take a look at what they did. If they lived in perma-nent settlements, they also knew how to preserve their food, but I will only deal with storage as a matter of interest, because the purpose of this book is to keep your belly full enough to get you home.

The best way to remember something is to have heart-and-hand knowledge, as opposed to "head" knowledge, and a good way to get that is to actually work with it. To appreciate what we discuss here as food, I've included recipes here and there that will let you enjoy the full potential of various foodstuffs. There is no way to forecast what cooking facilities you might have in a survival situation, so I'll give "kitchen" recipes just so you can try them and will remember what's good to eat; you'll need to do the best you can with what you have in the wilderness. Except for most acorns and some veggies, most of these plant foods can be eaten raw and on the run if you have to. In fact, there is a school of thought that holds raw food is better for you. Except for the need to kill microbes or parasites and to soften very fibrous food, raw may well be better because some vitamins are degraded by heat or leached away in hot water.

REGIONAL FAVORITES:
EXCELLENT SOURCES WHEN YOU'RE IN THE AREA

The following sections attempt to present edible plants suitable for survival, some of which are likely to be found all over the North American continent almost any time of year. As a practical matter, it was considered that the common wild foods the reader knows and understands are preferable to the myriad less-common plants that would require considerable study to remember and recognize, and the more common they are, the earlier they appear in this book.

Having said that, there are many easy foods growing in specific areas which within their venue are really good to know about but which may be geographically specific. So useful are they in their region, they are worthy of note, and I'll mention them in the context of their common geographic occurrence. You never know where that little Cessna will run out of fuel.

So here's a hearty *bon appétit.*

CATTAILS
The Found-Everywhere, Used-for-Everything Gourmet Survival Provision

I'll start with one of my favorite survival foods, which has been a staple of both Native American and rural European diets since prehistoric times. It's a favorite of mine for survival because it is found literally all over the world, virtually every part of the plant is edible at some time, and at least one part is edible at any given time of year that you find it—plus it's useful for shelter and other purposes. It is a good example of a food that is all around you. It's a virtual shmoo plant: the common cattail. It's not just for decorating autumn barn dances anymore—it's what's for dinner. If the only thing you take to heart from this book is that cattails will feed you, it could save your life.

The cattail is a survival gimme. *Typha latifolia,* the common cattail, or one of its varieties, will be found all over the Northern Hemisphere. There is everything to like about this plant: it's all edible (and tasty!), easy to identify, and easy to harvest. This makes it both a fine staple and an excellent survival food.

If I had to choose between surviving for a spell, barehanded, near a pond with catfish or one with cattails, I'd probably opt for the cattails, and not just because they are easier to catch with your hands. Sure, catfish are tasty and nutritious, but they're only one kind of food; cattails provide many kinds of meals—also tasty and nutritious—plus you can lay up a supply for winter or for travel. They provide medicine, clothing, and shelter to boot. One of the greatest points in their favor is that you may find them anywhere in moist soil or standing water . . . yes, even around a good catfish pond.

Some dozen species of this grass (despite its looks, it's a grass, but then so is bamboo) grow just about universally in the Northern Hemisphere and Australia, the most common and largest being *Typha latifolia*. All perennials, they spread out in favorable habitats, creating an incredibly dense food resource because virtually every part of the plant is edible. And not just "edible" as in goat fodder that only Euell Gibbons could love, but tasty and very nutritious fare, from the buckwheat-like, high-protein pollen at the top to the vitamin-rich shoots, stalks, and young flowers in the middle to the starchy, high-carbohydrate rhizome network in the soil. Some part is edible at every time of year, and it's always relatively easy to harvest, even barehanded. In spring, the first young shoots (corms) are tasty raw or cooked. As the shoots grow up, they are peeled and used like asparagus. Later, the female part of the flower (looks like a hotdog at the end of the stalk) may be boiled when immature and eaten like miniature corn on the cob.

The tough, fibrous root is edible any time of year (best in late fall/winter). Thoroughly clean them and pound chunks in a container of water to separate the starch, which may be collected by filtering or letting it settle, or boiling it down. Reportedly, you can dry the roots and then mill them for flour, which I have not tried, but the starch water you simply pound out acts very much like corn starch when added as a gravy thickener.

There is probably no other pollen on the planet as easy to harvest by the pound as cattail, and there are so many tasty things to do with this fine, flour-like staple. The male part, the spike on top of the hotdog, has an incredible amount of pollen, which can be shaken off into a bag and used as flour, boiled for a porridge or gruel, or roasted and added to meatloaf. And it is very high in protein, as is most pollen.

Considered objectively, the cattail would be the king of wild plants, and not just because it's one of the few grasses with a worthwhile root (actually a rhizome, an underground lateral stalk). Native Americans, for example, didn't consider the cattail as a food of last resort. It was a go-to culinary staple for many dishes, including desserts. It grew so well naturally that they didn't have to cultivate it.

Preserved *Typha* starch found on grinding stones in Paleolithic digs across Europe indicates that cattails were a common staple tens of thousands of years ago and would seem to indicate they ground the rhizomes before leaching or roasting them. Cattails thrive all over Europe. I've never seen really big forsaken stands there, because the folks eat 'em up. The early-season corms and tender young stalks are peeled and boiled and called "Cossack asparagus." They're excellent with a hollandaise sauce at home; in the woods, you can just graze. Depending on the cleanliness of the water, you may want to only eat raw above the waterline.

The best beds of cattails I've seen, though, have been in North America, probably because few people since the Native Americans and frontiersmen have molested them. They could be an immense resource if we'd quit draining our wetlands. How immense? There is actually a Cattail Research Center at Syracuse University, which cited some stunning numbers: they could harvest some 140 tons of rhizomes per acre per year (about 10 times a decent potato crop), which would yield 32 tons of dry cattail flour. Compare those numbers with spuds or GMO corn!

SURE WORKED FOR ME . . .

As kids in the Pacific Northwest, my best buddy Gilbert and I used to go "cattail camping." The rules we evolved allowed us to carry only matches, salt, a poncho between us, jackknives, a #10 can to carry/cook in, a Red Ryder BB gun, and later a mail-order "Bowie" knife bought from an ad in *Boy's Life* with strawberry-picking money. Plus one 5-cent candy bar each to get us there, which was usually just a mile or two into the woods in back of the Johnsons' farm. Obviously, we ate a lot of crawdads and tweetie birds, plus the occasional poached fish—and cattails. Lots of cattails. Only once did we eat anything that gave us a bellyache (never knew just what it was, but 20 years later my hair started falling out, too). Cattails often ended up being the staple part of our groceries and a good part of our shelter. During fire season, we were vegans until Gib read an article about cooking with a tin-foil reflector. Nobody knew what sushi was then. But cattails are good raw, too, even just the pounded-out starch water if you're genuinely hungry!

WINTER AND SPRING, ROOTS AND CORMS

Keeping in mind that you can dry and keep cattail pollen and starch to use all year, let's do a calendar-based recipe review of cattail cooking. It's honestly haute cuisine when done right in a kitchen and tolerable victuals in the wild because it starts good, and by the time you have putzed with it under aboriginal conditions, odds are that you'll have worked up an appetite. Cattail products may be too labor intensive for the supermarket, but what's that got to do with a survivalist, yesterday or today?

For a root starch, cattails contain a fair amount of gluten, which is good news if you want to make flatbread or tortillas, or need it to hang together because you don't have utensils. In the woods, we just washed and peeled the roots, cut them up, and pounded them with water in the can with a blunt stick until the starch washed out and then, best we could, strained out the fiber, let the good stuff settle, and poured off the water. You can also split the root and scrape out the starchy part, which is still fibrous, and wash the starch out of that. Depending on your setting, you can wash, cut up, and dry the roots; then pound them as fine as you can; put them in a cloth; and boil the starch out.

Our best recipe was to boil it down until it got about like porridge and then add pollen, if in season, until it got thick, about like biscuit dough. We'd put a wad of that on a forked stick and roast it in the fire like a marshmallow or stick biscuit, or we'd cook any consistency from batter on up on a hot rock. Once, we mashed in a lot of blackberries, and that was a pudding you wouldn't have to apologize for, anywhere. In even a frontier kitchen, of course, you would have all kinds of options for preparing and cooking. The starch can be quite sweet, but different varieties of cattail, in different growing conditions, will vary in flavor and quantity. Best starch collecting is in late fall and winter, when it's stored in the rhizome.

Some people think it tastes like mashed potatoes if seasoned the same; some think it tastes like poi. Peeled and the inner core thinly sliced, tender shoots can be fried and taste like new potatoes to some palates. As with most bland-flavored starchy foods, adding seasoning of choice can really help.

Last year's seeds are also edible once you burn the fluff, but they're so small I never have seriously bothered. I've also read that East Coast Indian cooks mashed and boiled the roots and then boiled the juice down to a thick syrup, but I never tried that either.

SPRING AND SUMMER:
CORMS, SHOOTS, AND SPIKES

With spring, you can pretend you are the legendary panda who walks into a bar, eats shoots, and leaves. The pointed little corms that sprout up from the rhizome can be broken off and, if the water is clean, eaten on the spot. Some folks think they taste like cucumbers or zucchini. Once these corms grow into an upward shoot, that shoot can be peeled and eaten raw. The easiest way to harvest shoots once they break water is to grab the stalk like it was a grass stem you wanted to chew on and pull straight up. The crisp, white lower part is what you want, just like on any other grass stem. On the upper portion of a shoot, peel away the outer layers until you get to the crisp and tender inner parts; then just pretend it is asparagus. Boil or sauté it, can it, or pickle it, just like you would asparagus. Generations of Cossacks can't be wrong. Raw, some folks think this part tastes like mild celery.

Usually around the end of June, you can get tender inner stalks, immature "corncob" flowers, and pollen all at the same time from different plants in the same stand. Peel the leaves away from the developing flower spike, boil, and eat like very small corn on the cob. It may be the power of suggestion, but they tend to taste a little like corn. The male shoots at the very top, which produce pollen, can also be boiled and the soft parts eaten early on, before the larger female parts really have started to form. In short, any tender part can be eaten raw or cooked, any time you can get it. Think salads, stir-fries, and casseroles.

MIDSUMMER KNIGHT'S DREAM: A CATTAIL SHOOT

You can peel and eat the shoots well into the summer: pick the largest shoots that haven't begun to flower and pull straight up. Peel and toss all outside layers that are not tender. The ratio of food to fiber varies with the size of the shoot: for efficiency, go for the biggest ones that are still tender.

By the end of June in most areas, seed heads will mature and pollen will come. It's the most worthwhile pollen I've found that doesn't have to be harvested by bees. Just bend the top over into a paper bag, hold the bag closed, and shake. In a good stand, if the wind has not robbed it, you can get pounds per hour.

It's yellow and very fine like flour—I'd guess about 100 mesh or finer—so it doesn't have to be milled before using it to upgrade or extend flour. It's quick and easy protein for a knight errant or other woods traveler, with a nutty/corny/buckwheaty flavor to it. Like the starch, it's a good component or extender for all kinds of recipes from mush to meatloaf, from soup to cinnamon rolls, from casseroles to cornmeal pudding. It gives a yellow cast if mixed with wheat flour for attractive cookies and muffins. Both pollen and starch work well with other ingredients, and although the starch may be sweet, it's available and extractible year 'round, any time you need carbs.

Once you and your consort start using it around your cabin, you'll find yourself substituting this pollen for flour in all kinds of breads, biscuits, cakes, and cookies—just like our frontier forebears.

And another thing: on the frontier, when the rib sent you out for venison or a mess of fish, even if you got skunked, you never had to return without *something* for the pot if you had cattails!

FAVORITE RECIPE:
POLLEN PANCAKES

If you like buckwheat cakes, you'll kill for these:

1 cup flour
1 cup cattail pollen
2 teaspoons baking powder
1 teaspoon salt
2 eggs
2 cups of milk
½ cup honey
¼ cup oil

Mix dry ingredients in bowl. Add eggs, oil, honey, and milk, and mix well. If the batter is too thick, add a little water. Cook on lightly greased griddle that will dance a drop of water. You did make maple or birch syrup this winter, didn't ya?

MEDICINE, SHELTER, AND UTILITY

One caution: *some people are allergic to the fluff on cattails.* It can trigger asthma or cause skin rashes on contact, much like wool does to some folks. Fluff, subject to individual allergies, is an excellent insulator for clothing and quilts, and was used for futons in Asia prior to cotton. Ground raw or macerated, the root pulp makes a poultice, much the same as a potato or onion poultice, for cuts, burns, stings, and bruises. Dried tops can be used as a punk to carry fire or fluffed for the best tinder we've ever found to catch a spark. Dried flower heads dipped in fat make great torches. Cut green, dried, and resoaked, cattail leaves make baskets and mats (some were found in Nevada that were more than 10,000 years old), hats, ponchos, or thatch. Dried stalks serve for myriad light dowel purposes.

POSITIVE IDENTIFICATION

Some plants with the same wet venue bear a superficial resemblance to cattails, and some are either inedible or downright toxic members of the iris family, for instance. But positive identification is simple: if it doesn't have a cattail at the top, *then it's not a cattail!* Even in a hard winter in the Rocky Mountains, there will be the dead-standing round stalks, usually with tattered, fuzzy remnants of the cattail at the top to guide you. Follow only these stalks into the mud to find the rhizome it grows from. If there are remnants of a seedpod, then it's not cattail and likely iris—which means it is toxic. Since plants that look similar to the untrained eye can grow side by side, if your hand can't follow the obvious cattail stalk to the rhizome, then move on.

If there is a universal survival food, it may well be the cattail. Photo: Wikipedia.

ACORNS
Mighty Meals from
Tiny Acorns Grow

I only deal with the genus *Quercus* here, which comprises some 600+ varieties of oak worldwide, and not the related *Lithocarpus,* native to Asia, which is actually a beech although it does have wee "acorns."

Acorns are a great food resource, and you can harvest or find them almost all year except for spring and early summer. That's the good news. The bad news is, they generally are not a food you can graze and eat on the run: their high tannic acid content must first be leached away, and that requires either long-term soaking or short-term boiling. But when you have the time and space to do either, they are surely worth the effort. They are a great source of carbohydrates (call that f-u-e-l) and are thus a very good trail food to stock up on before a trek back to civilization or to lay in for a future season. The tannic acid must be dealt with not only because its bitterness makes acorns unpalatable, but also because it also makes them inedible.

Even though you have to deal with the tannic acid, oaks of myriad species are native all over the world, and folks all over the world have always used them as a dietary mainstay. Like the oak trees themselves, which grow as the mighty oak of legend, or the scrub oak bush of the desert Southwest, acorns come in every size and shape as well.

Despite their varying styles, acorns are hard to confuse with anything else. First, you find them hanging from or on the ground beneath an oak tree. And again, although there are hundreds of natural variations on the theme, an oak leaf of most species will tend to be recognizable as an oak leaf. And even if not in the leaf litter, at its base you will find last year's "hats" from acorns. Many oaks are "live," i.e., they keep their leaves until they are displaced by the next spring's new leaves. The only other shrub a person might confuse with the scrub oak is the jojoba bush, both native to the desert. The distinct difference is like that between the acorn and any other tree nut: the acorn wears a distinctive "hat," and the jojoba does not. Also, the jojoba seed is three-sided, not round. The jojoba is about 50 percent indigestible wax and is a strong laxative; thus, it is inedible (but it makes great soap).

Detoxing bitter acorns is a simple task. Even if you could get past the bitter taste, the tannic acid can give you a bellyache at best to raging diarrhea at worst. Over time you can expect kidney damage if you do not properly leach the tannic acid. *Do not try to develop a tolerance for it.* Although cows and horses can develop an unhealthy taste for oak leaves and acorns that can lead to ailments, pigs are immune: acorns of all varieties are a nutritious staple of the feral pigs that have taken over a lot of North American wild country. To make into people food, fixing acorns is a small but necessary hassle compared to the valuable product you end up with.

After-season ground pickups may either be bug-eaten or moldy. It's OK to eat after most insects and grubs, if they have left you anything, but beware moldy nuts and grains, especially if the mold is black or purple. In late winter you may even find some starting to sprout, and they're OK. By the time the sprout starts to form a leaf and the nut is turning green, however, they're past salvaging because the carbs you want have been converted. Some oaks are evergreen; some acorns develop in six months; some grow in 24 months. Different varieties often grow side-by-side, and, yes, they sometimes hybridize. Although oaks grow virtually all over, they have largely overlapping venues, so you never know what you will find. Plan to work with what you have. It's all good.

Although they have a sweet aftertaste, acorns have a low sugar content, making them good in stews and breads of all types. They are rich in complex carbs, minerals, and vitamins. They contain a lot of oil but are lower in fat than most other nuts. And they are a good source of fiber.

Different varieties of acorns have different levels of tannin. They range from the Emory oak of the southwestern United States from Arizona to Texas and into Mexico, which is so mild it can be used like any other nut, to some others with very bitter acorns, requiring repeated processing to make them edible. There is a gigantic Emory oak in Yarnell, Arizona, at about 5,000 feet that usually produces prodigious harvests of the typical smaller acorns, and I have eaten them on the spot, although I prefer them roasted or as meal, with no leaching. Acorns vary widely. Like most nuts, acorns of all types benefit from roasting, although in the wild I wouldn't bother until I had them completely leached.

Taste what you find and see; the less-bitter ones will be the best to fix to eat, when you have a choice. And you will know when they have been "fixed," because they are no longer bitter.

Generally, the best acorns to harvest are those of the white oaks, such as the swamp oak, Oregon white oak, and burr oak, because as a group they contain less-bitter tannin. Luckily, nearly all acorns can be made usable with simple leaching, which renders them nutty, sweet, and very healthy.

I have found it's a lot more profitable to coarsely grind or at least mash the acorns before leaching. In the woods, you can tie them in a cloth and leave them in a fast-running stream for a day or two until they are no longer bitter. If you can heat water, boil them through several changes of water. A lot of old books say to boil them in ashes, but I could never see any difference in results in terms of how fast it goes, except for mashing them first, to give the water access to the meat. Wet acorn meal will tend to quickly mold, so dry it thoroughly if you intend to keep it.

Bring the acorns or acorn meal to a boil in plenty of water and continue boiling for about 15 minutes. The water will turn brown as the tannic acid is leached from the kernels. Throw out the water and replace it with fresh water. Reboil the acorns, throwing out the brown water several times if necessary until the water is clear. The boiling process when using whole acorns takes two or three hours, though the time varies with the amount of tannic acid in the acorns. When you are finished, the acorns will no longer taste bitter and will have turned a darker brown, to a chocolate color. The taste test will tell you when you are done with the particular type of acorns you have.

In the wilderness, you can crack and mash acorns at the same time with no tools. Place the acorn on flat rock A and crack it with flat-sided rock B. Remove the shell (and cork-like husk that some varieties have) and proceed to mash the acorn as flat as you can so it will leach efficiently.

Even leached, different species have a slightly different taste. The most common characterization one hears is "chestnuts." Other descriptions vary, from "like hazelnuts" (filberts) to "like sunflower seeds." They tend to have a slightly bitter initial taste, especially if you were not diligent about the leaching, and a sweet aftertaste—like chestnuts. To me they taste like chestnuts, but not quite so buttery. (Yes, I ate a lot of chestnuts 60 years ago as a kid, before they almost all died from chestnut blight.)

In the woods, when thoroughly leached, you can dry or roast acorns and eat; or you can dry them to a damp meal, press into cakes and roast on a flat rock, and eat. A little salt if you have it works wonders.

At home, run the shelled acorns through a kitchen grinder and place the ground acorns in a large crock or glass bowl. Then add boiling water to cover and let stand an hour, stirring several times. Drain and discard the brownish water. Taste the meal. It should have a bit of a bitter tang and then taste sweet as you chew it. Continue leaching out the tannin until the meal is mild tasting. Press and squeeze the meal in a cloth, removing as much of the water (and tannin) as possible. Spread the damp meal out to dry, stirring it a few times to get rid of lumps and expose the damp meal.

To prepare acorn flour at home, run the leached whole or coarsely ground nuts through a food grinder or blender. If the flour still is damp, dry it in the oven first. Then regrind the flour, if needed, to the fineness you want. Use it in breads, either by itself or with other flours. You can make some surprisingly decent flour in the woods if you have one flat rock and another with a flat side, rubbing the meal between them.

Like I mentioned before, it's worthwhile to be able to relate to a "wild" food you have actually cooked with, and experiencing something is one of the best ways to remember it. So I'd suggest that, at the least, you grind up some meal or mealy flour, properly leach it, and cook something tasty. You can make a cooked mush with the meal, much as you would use cornmeal, or cut it about half with cornmeal and put that mush in a bread-loaf pan and cool it. When cold, slice it, fry in butter, and hit it with butter and maple syrup, jam, or your

Acorns have been feeding folks for ages, and you'll find them all over. Today, as a rule, your only competition in the woods will be animals. Photo: Wikipedia.

The best way to tell if an acornn is really an acorn is whether it has a hat or turban on. If not, it is not an acorn. Photo: Wikipedia.

favorite pancake condiment. A little cattail flour helps to make it hang together better.

Your favorite recipe for corn dodgers is also directly adaptable to acorn meal, and they also make good tortillas if you do them a little thick. And if you like grits, acorn meal is for you. Cook it and eat it the same ways: with gravy, jam, or whatever you like. It is similar to but richer tasting than corn grits. Overall, I think you will find acorn meal to be mild flavored, if properly leached, and self-sweetening. It can be added to breads or cakes where you might add nuts or sun-flower seeds. It's tasty there but may make some breads a little heavy (add a little more yeast).

Because acorns are the most common wild nut, I have dealt with them separately here. See also the separate entries on other wild nuts. A reminder on the desert jojoba nut: these are native to the American Southwest and will grow in juxtaposition with species of small scrub oak. They are not toxic as such, but their large component of indigestible wax makes them inedible and has a strong laxative effect on most people. I do not consider them as food. *If a nut does not have the typical "turban" or "hat" on the stem end, it is not an acorn.*

CLOVER
Lucky Food No Matter
How Many Leaves

Clover is another fast field food that's a real gimme, and it's underfoot and underrated. Clover is native all over Europe, North and South America at higher elevations, and South Africa. Most commonly encountered these days are the widely cultivated clovers—white clover (*Trifolium repens*) and red clover (*Trifolium pratense)*—but people have used clover as food and animal forage since prehistoric times.

Clover (*Trifolium*), or trefoil, is a genus of some 300 species of plants in the leguminous pea family *Fabaceae*. The genus now grows all over, with the greatest variety being found in the temperate Northern Hemisphere. The common clovers are small annual, biennial, or short-lived perennial herbaceous plants, variously suited to different climes.

On the trek west, wagon-train pioneers relied on native clover as a staple for themselves and their draft animals, prized in particular for its ability to prevent scurvy because of its vitamin C content. Indigenous North American people—such as the Cherokee, Iroquois, Mohegan, Delaware, and Algonquin—have used clover as food and in folk medicine for centuries. Clover has a high level of the vitamins usually associated with green vegetables and a high mineral content as well. Compared to other leafy vegetables, clover is also high in protein.

Being widely distributed and abundant, clovers are another "weed" that can be both a shelf-ready staple and an excellent survival food of opportunity. Although traditionally used in sandwiches, clover is not easy to digest raw because it is relatively fibrous, but it can be juiced or boiled for 5–10 minutes for greens or added to any dish using greens, as it has been since pre-history. Dried flower heads and seedpods can also be ground into nutritious flour and mixed with other foods. Dried flower heads can be steeped in hot water for a healthy, tasty tea.

At home, white-clover flour is sometimes sprinkled over cooked foods, such as boiled rice. When used in soups, the leaves are usually picked when they are most tender, before the plant flowers. The roots are also edible but fibrous, so they need to be cooked if possible. If you are foraging when clover is in bloom, the flowers may be the tastiest part of the plant, and they do very well stir-fried, sautéed, tossed in salads, or cooked as greens. They are also less fibrous, so they make a better "grab-growl-and-go" snack if you have to keep moving. They actually make a good pocket food, for a green, as the flower heads do not all mash together in your pocket, and they are easy to strip off the plant without even breaking your stride.

Rare is the country kid who has not picked the flower heads and pulled the center flowers out to suck their nectar!

Note on red clover: A massively cultivated forage crop the world over, red clover (*Trifolium pretense)* is also regarded as edible by humans, as are all clovers. However, some sources suggest caution on the part of any female with hormonal issues or any person taking anticoagulants, regarding the use of red clover due to its activity on estrogen receptors, and to its possible coumarin derivatives. Aside from its unmistakable large, deep-pink flower heads, red clover also tends to grow taller and with more branches than white clover. It is a premier source of honey.

Note on wood sorrel: Common wood sorrel is a plant from the genus *Oxalis* and is the only close mimic of clover, as it grows with the almost identical three leaves. It is usually found in the shade, thus its name. Sorrel and clover are interchangeably called "shamrocks" in folklore, but they are distinctly different. The flower of the sorrel just looks like a wee single white flower, whereas clover flower heads are clusters of many individual flowers. The dead giveaway is that sorrel is distinctly tart, like rhubarb, because of the oxalic acid that it contains, as is also found in rhubarb and spinach. The amounts of oxalic acid in rhubarb stalks, spinach, and sorrel are not considered toxic; *the amount in rhubarb leaves is toxic.* Sorrel,

White clover after a rain. Photo: Wikipedia.

White clover, *Trifolium repens*, aka "Dutch clover," is probably the king of clover for grazing as people food. Native to Europe, it is now found all over the globe. Photo: Wikipedia.

Oxalis Montana, the common wood sorrel you are likely to find in North America, is tart but edible. It prefers the acid soil and shade of the woods, while clover likes clay soil and sunshine. It is not related to clover. Note the distinctive single flower. Photo: Wikipedia.

therefore, is edible but best used as a seasoning in greens. There is also a four-leaf sorrel native to Mexico, with a lemony flavor.

What's not to like about clover? It's found all over, and bazillions of rabbits can't be wrong.

JERUSALEM ARTICHOKE
Never Seen Jerusalem, Never Been an Artichoke: But *Good!*

This delightful tuber (*Helianthus tuberosus*) is not an artichoke but a native sunflower and has nothing to do with Jerusalem. Containing almost no starch (it stores its carbs as inulin), when boiled this tuber does have a flavor that reminds you of an artichoke, but you can take your pick of theories on how the name came about.

Unmolested, the gnarly root tuber of this perennial will continue to grow into a large root mass a few inches below the soil, weighing several pounds, and is easy to harvest from the wild in soft soil, or to grow. The Jerusalem artichoke has been marketed as a sunchoke, and various cultivars are available in some seed catalogs. They have even been promoted in pyramid schemes as the next save-the-planet plant for food and fuel. In Germany, they are used to make booze called *Topinambur* and have been promoted as a source of fuel alcohol. They give some people gas, but is that a bad thing? Not working in favor of the species in the supermarket are its gnarly appearance (rather like ginger root) and the fact that most potential buyers, except for gourmet cooks and country folk, don't know what to do with it.

It has excellent nutritional value (particularly high in minerals) and minimal starch, and it will substitute in most recipes that call for boiled potato: soups, stews, casseroles, or just boiled and dressed with butter or gravy. It can be shredded as a nice addition to salads and makes the best water-chestnut substitute there is in stir-fry recipes. It can even be dried and milled for flour, like potatoes. The tops can be used like corn stalks for silage or animal forage.

Preparation is not particularly hard but requires a different technique than spuds. Since you probably got it for free, you can afford

The leaves and tall stalk of the Jerusalem artichoke are similar to a sunflower, but the long rooot tubers are the food. iStockphoto.com/Andris Tkachenko.

In the daisy family, the bright yellow flowers can make patches of Jerusalem artichokes easy to spot. Photo: Wikipedia.

to be a little wasteful and use a sharp knife to cut away the gnarly outer part if you don't like it. But the skin is very thin, and the only reason to peel it is for esthetics. If you're good with a stiff vegetable brush, you can get them clean, and the little eyes usually come off during this scrubbing. I have found that a strong stream of water works best (at home I use a yard-sale Waterpik). The skin tends to fall off when cooked as well.

If you are growing them on purpose, they produce better if dug up and replanted every year and will grow from seed or a small fragment of tuber . . . so only plant them where you want them. Plant it in a corner of your garden or a moist field where you don't plan to till, and it will always be there. The plant grows 7–8 feet tall and looks like a small sunflower, which makes them easy to spot in the wild.

In their natural habitats, they tend to congregate in meadows and river bottoms. During bloom, the bright yellow flowers of a good stand can be seen a long way off. In the winter, the tall stalks remain, with the dry flower heads being worked by birds. In farm country, they tend to congregate along fencerows.

In soft soil, a good tug on the base of the stalk may bring up a root mass. If you don't mind some extra minerals, you can brush the dirt off and eat it as is. It tastes something like a raw potato crossed with an apple. Crunchy. You can eat it raw, boil it, or roast it. I encased some in clay once and roasted them, and the skin came off with the clay, like feathers coming off a quail. They get soft and transparent when cooked but seem to be perfectly digestible raw. They are likely to be found in most temperate zones, and they are not frost sensitive. And they are solid enough when you find some that you can stock up on a quantity to carry. These tubers are good any time of year but sweetest in the fall.

PURSLANE
Pretty, Succulent, Delicious

Purslane (*Portulaca olearacea*) isn't just some deer fodder only a Sasquatch could love. It's a juicy, crisp succulent that grows close to the ground, quickly if unmolested, and lavishly if in good soil with adequate water, although it also grows in bum soil and through drought. Interestingly, it's pressure from high-class yuppie restaurants and not "survivalists" that is finally bringing purslane to the marketplace and menu. Purslane has six times more vitamin E than spinach and seven times more beta-carotene than carrots. The stems are rich in vitamin C and contain glutathione, riboflavin, potassium, magnesium, phosphorus, tryptophan, and omega-3 fatty acids. You read that right: omega-3 fatty acids, which protect your heart and rich folks get from salmon. It's best to pick early or late in the day or after a good rain. The best part is, it's tasty.

To me, raw it tastes very much like Miner's lettuce, as grows along the West Coast of the United States. Others think it tastes like a slightly tart-spicy lettuce. You can pull it up by the roots and continue to march as you graze. In cooked recipes, it's hard to tell from spinach as far as taste. Makes a great salad green, or you can cook it as a potherb. Sauté it as a side dish in olive oil with some chopped onions and garlic. You can blanch it and freeze it if you intend to cook it. It is a superior substitute for spinach or chard in most recipes, as it does not have their bothersome (to some) oxalic acid. It is becoming popular in upscale restaurants.

Long a popular veggie in southern Europe, purslane was assumed to have been brought to North America by Europeans, either on purpose or as a hitchhiker. Recent discoveries in eastern

Purslane is easy to identify, with its round, smooth stems growing flat to the ground; its wedge-shaped, succulent leaves; and its small, yellow flowers. Young plants have a green stem, which turns red as the plant gets older. For best flavor and texture, go for the young stuff. But it's all good and good for you. Photo: Wikipedia.

Discrete yellow flowers produce tiny black seeds that spread this prolific annual. Photo: Wikipedia.

Canada indicate, however, that Native Americans were making use of purslane in pre-Columbian times. Some 40 varieties are cultivated in various places, but they all look like purslane. The first time I saw purslane I thought, "That's so pretty—it has to be good to eat," and it was. In a "civilized" setting, don't harvest it where some unappreciative dummy has sprayed it with herbicide.

PURSLANE RECIPES

Gourmet recipes using purslane abound, but the quick answer is to use it every which way—raw or cooked, sautéed or boiled, stir-fried or in spinach recipes. Here's my quick and dirty salad: wash the plant in cold water, removing roots and heavy stems, until you have about 4 cups. Combine 1/4 cup catsup, 1/4 cup mayonnaise, and 1/2 teaspoon vinegar, and mix well with purslane. Slice or shred one hard-boiled egg and about an ounce of sharp cheddar cheese. You can stop there, or if you have a good handful of shelled crawdad tails, put them on top, or substitute small shrimp. You can take it from there, using purslane for about any purpose you would use any green veggie.

It's almost worth getting lost in the woods, just for an excuse to eat purslane.

DANDELION
One Man's Travail Is Another Man's Trekking Treat

The ubiquitous weed dandelion (*Taraxacum officinale)* actually has many varieties, including a number of cultivars raised as food. The entire plant is edible, but the roots are strongly diuretic. The common dandelion is an import from Europe, although there is a native, and endangered, California dandelion. Often considered a great pest because of the rate at which it invades and propagates in lawns, gardens, and fields, the dandelion is actually a beneficial weed, posing no danger except for its propensity to take over, and it actually improves the soil.

The dandelion is a good survival food because of its universal growing habit and the fact it is entirely edible and high in vitamins and minerals, especially iron and potassium, which you especially need in times of stressful activity.

The name comes from the French *dent-de-lion*, meaning lion's tooth, in reference to the sharply cut leaves. Groundskeepers call it by many names, none flattering. Likewise, "piss-a-bed" is an English folk-name for this plant, in reference to the diuretic properties of the root. They have been used by humans for food and as an herb since the dawn of history. The hollow stems can be used as a (somewhat fragile) drinking straw.

The early spring leaves make good (if slightly bitter) salad greens or potherbs, and a good component for omelets and quiche. At home, most cooked dandelion recipes start with blanching the dandelions: wash clean, discard any bug-eaten or brown leaves, boil in salted water for a good minute, and then quench in ice water. When cooled, drain and proceed with the recipe, or you can freeze them. If

Unmolested and in good soil, the dandelion can grow to surprising heights. Some cultivars have very broad leaves, easily blanched. When mowed in a lawn, adaptable dandelion will bloom at 1 inch tall. Photo: Wikipedia.

(Inset) The bright yellow florets, comprising many individual flowers, grow on a single pinkish stem and make the common dandelion easy to identify. Leaves, stems, and flowers are all edible. Photo: Wikipedia.

growing dandelions on purpose, tie up the leaves around the flower stalk, and then cut off the floret. The inner leaves will blanch white, as would endive, and these dandelion leaves will be mild and tender, with an endive sort of flavor. As a crop, they will get more bitter due to heat, drought, or the lateness of the season.

The flowers make a wine that looks and tastes rather like beer. The root can be roasted and ground to make a chicory-like coffee substitute (which I don't really care for, but I don't like chicory either).

Many health benefits are ascribed to dandelion, but remember that the root is a diuretic; when I was a kid we would dig dandelion roots and sell them to buyers for the pharmaceutical companies, such as the F.C. Taylor Fur Company. If nothing else, gather leaves for your rabbits and you'll have friends for life. Early dandelion leaves are a popular "spring tonic" green among country folk. Cooking takes the edge off the strong flavor (which is like bitter lettuce), and like most greens, the young and tender leaves are the best. They get more bitter as they get close to the stem and have more milky sap. But in the woods or on the run, they're a healthy grab-and-go food.

A RECIPE TO REMEMBER DANDELIONS BY

Dandelions are an excellent component of many dishes from salads to casseroles, but they can be a good stand-alone side dish. Blanch, drain, and cut in about 1-inch pieces. Sautee in butter with a little garlic, salt, and light pepper. They're good just like that!

BULRUSHES
A Neighbor to the
Ubiquitous Cattail

Bulrushes are known by two formal names, *Schoenoplectus tabernaemontani* and *Scirpus validus*. This flowering plant in the sedge family is also called soft-stem bulrush and great bulrush. It grows all over the world in moist or wet areas or in shallow water. It varies in appearance and size by where it grows, and there are even decorative cultivars. The one shown is representative.

A perennial herb, bulrush grows from a long rhizome system, and many parts are edible, including the tender young shoots, pollen, seeds, and root stalk. The first three can be eaten as you graze, but rhizomes, although a great potato substitute, take a long time (hours) to bake. Back at the ranch, they can also be washed, dried, and pounded into flour. As with cattail shoots, the cleanliness of the water where they are harvested is a consideration if you cannot wash them.

Right: Found the world over in wet soil or shallow water, the great bulrush has many edible parts. Photo: Wikipedia.

PINE
Offers a Lot More Than Piñon Nuts and Coffins

At first blush, one might think that the primary benefit of pine as a survival food would be that it is hard to confuse it with anything else. That's true, of course, although among the more than 100 species of pine, there is a wide variety of shapes and sizes.

The most well-known food product of the pine is the pine nut, which in some species is large, well formed, and delicious, and a staple of European and Native American cooking. A consideration of pine seeds is that, although all are edible, most are very small and you have to be there at the right season to harvest them, unless you have the time and facilities to rob a squirrel stash of cones and dry them out off-season. It has been my experience that, among pines in general, a more reliable seasonal food is the pollen-bearing male anthers you find in the spring. They are easy to identify in the spring; they look like clusters of little fuzzy candles and are covered with dusty pollen. Eat them whole but pick carefully so as not to lose the pollen, which is very high in protein.

But the most reliable food from a pine tree is, well, *the pine tree*. The soft, moist (downright juicy in the early spring), white inner cambium layer of bark is edible and very high in vitamins A and C. When a chunk of bark is removed, all you have to do is scrape the white cambium layer off the inside. It is not "pitchy" at all, and in some white pines it is very sweet to the taste. It can be eaten raw in slices as a snack or dried and ground to flour for a thickener in stews and soups or an extender in casseroles or baked dishes. The Finns bake a traditional *pettuleipa* pine-bark bread. It does smell like pine when baking but to me has no identifiable pine flavor. So into eating

Above: The rough cone of the single-leaf, one of several piñon pines, may hide an in-season banquet. Piñon pines grow at higher elevation, in a lower, branching style than the various pines cut for lumber. Photo Wikipedia.

Above left: The ponderosa pine is of considerable economic importance in the American West. Many other pines are smaller, but all are of survival importance as food.

Above right: Pine needles vary in size and shape, but all look like pine when compared to other conifers, and all have the distinctive "pine" aroma. Photos: Wikipedia.

pine-tree products were the Adirondack Indians, their name is derived from the Mohawk word *atirú:taks*, which means "tree eaters."

The needles can be eaten themselves (do not swallow anything but well-chewed and tender young buds), and they make a good tea that is high in vitamins A and C, if brewed in boiling water.

Note on pine needles: There are veterinary and medical references to pine needles causing spontaneous abortion in animals and humans. However, deer will scrape bark and graze on young pine buds in winter and early spring, when they would be carrying, which might lead one to conclude the danger exists primarily from the mature needles.

The premium pine food, of course, is the pine nut. Some 20 species produce "nuts" (seeds) of economic importance, in North America comprising the three main varieties of pinyon pine. They are geographically specific to the Southwest, at elevations from 5,000–7,000 feet. They take more than a year to mature. If you find yourself in their venue at harvest time, don't miss them.

The primary survival resource of the pine, however, is still the inner bark, good any time; young needles, good any time; the new buds, good in the spring; and the male pollen spikes, good in the later spring. There are many species of pine native to North America, some found in almost every area. If you have a pine tree and a jackknife or a sharp rock, you have a meal.

NETTLES
Easy to Understand, Hard to Grasp

Nettles are a good resource as survival food, with the caveat that you must be able to cook them to kill the stinging hairs of the leaves and stalk. They are nutritious, but in a survival scenario, you don't need the hassle of (temporary) irritation. Some Brits eat raw nettles for sport. To each his own. One might be able to thoroughly maul the leaves and break all the stinging hairs, but I have never tried it.

Urtica dioica is a perennial found in the moist areas of Europe and North America. It requires moisture, and, if also given rich soil and cool temperatures such as in the Pacific Northwest, it grows in rank profusion to 7–8 feet tall. It is native to all U.S. states except Hawaii. It has long been used as a staple food component in the British Isles and Scandinavia, where it often grows in rich soil where old barns and outhouses once stood. Native Americans harvested the greens, primarily in the spring, before more friendly greens were available.

Probably best known for their use in the British nettle soup, nettles are suitable, when boiled, for any use where one could use spinach—plus numerous therapeutic uses for various ailments, even simply dried for making a healthy tea. Again, some say it tastes "like spinach." To me, it tastes a little like spinach with some green tea thrown in. As a cooked green, it has a very slightly bitter taste—not unlike a pot of spinach with a few dandelion greens added.

A great deal of scientific research has been done on the medicinal properties of the "stinging" nettle. The "stinging" part of the nettle contains acetylcholine, histamine, 5-HT, or serotonin, and possibly formic acid encased in fragile, pointed spines that penetrate the skin and release the irritants when the plant is gently brushed.

Many species are found in the temperate regions of Europe and North America, but this *Urtica dioica* is the food of choice and the most common. Photo: Wikipedia.

Close-up shows hollow "hairs" that produce the sting. None of the nettle varieties are truly dangerous except a rare species found only in New Zealand, or perhaps to people who have an individual allergy. Photo: Wikipedia.

Most folks get a simple rash. Rudely handled, the spines tend to break off ineffectually, thus the poet's advice to "grasp the nettle like a lad of mettle . . ." It is best harvested with gloves, although as noted in the United Kingdom they eat them raw in contests! Folk remedies abound to cure the stings; the best one I've come across is to briskly rub the affected area—immediately—with a handful of the leaves. Yeh, I know, "hair of the dog," but it works for me. The stinging can be intense if you really get into them, but on most folks it doesn't last long, compared to bee stings, poison oak, or similar hassles.

Some nettle connoisseurs only like the tender young tops, and if you are very careful you can pick parts without evident stinging hairs. In a good stand of nettles, there usually are plenty of plants if you want to harvest selectively.

The easy way to harvest a lot of them—with gloves—is to cut the stalk at the bottom, trim it up to where the good leaves start, hold the top in one hand, and strip downward with the other hand. They tend to sweep right off. You can blanch them and freeze them in plastic bags just like garden greens. They also can well and, being fairly acidic for a green, probably with relative safety. You can also add a tablespoon of vinegar to the jar before you put on the lids.

I have seen basket-type (loose) flexible cordage made from the fibers of the long stalks that have had the soft material boiled away. It was quite fine fiber. It did not look as if it would be strong enough for good rope, but in times past it has been grown in Europe for cordage, probably with a different or more specific method of twisting.

SMALL MALLOW
Tasty Leaves and Seeds

If you are not familiar with *Malva neglecta* and *Malva parviflora*, the most common varieties found in North America, I can see a question forming on your lips: the answer is yes. There is a relationship between this mucilaginous plant and the common marshmallow. The root from the marshland cousin (*Althaea officinalis*) of this mallow was used for its gooey sap as the basis for the original marshmallow confection, although now they are made with whipped gelatin. In some places, mallow is called "wild geranium," which it is not, because of the leaf shape. (Do not confuse the name with desert "mallow" [*sic*], which rather resembles a snapdragon plant with a flat orange flower and is toxic and especially irritating to the eyes.)

Originally from Europe but now found all over, mallow is also called "cheese plant," because its pea-sized seeds look like miniature green wheels of cheese. The small flowers vary from light pink to purple.

The whole plant is edible, although like most greens it is best when young and tender. It is a tasty component for salads or as a cooked green in suitable recipes. Its mucilaginous sap may remind you of okra. Very nutritious (a good source of calcium and magnesium, it also contains potassium, iron, selenium, and vitamins A and C), mallow leaves may be blanched and frozen or canned. The juice is used for various digestive disorders, for its mucilaginous polysaccharides that are much like aloe vera, or as a topical medicine. The nutlike, labor-intensive seeds are eaten in Europe.

An annual, mallow has one of the best tap roots in the business

This young small mallow is about the size for a salad. You can also pick the smaller new leaves from a large plant. If treated like a crop, it gets a few feet high, doesn't ask for much food or water. and still gives a good return on labor. Photo by Howard F. Schwartz, Colorado State University, courtesy www.forestryimages.org.

and is a real survivor. It has been studied as a crop for starving people who do not have resources to grow anything else. They certainly could do worse.

As a survival or trail food, the more tender leaves may be stripped and eaten as you go. If the seeds are in season, you can strip off a pocketful and eat them when you sit to rest.

LAMB'S QUARTER
Everyman's Herb

This plant (most common is *Chenopodium album)* thrives all over North and Central America. Grown as a crop by North American natives, iy is still grown for harvest in Mexico. The whole plant, including the seeds, is edible, but the tastiest part is the young, tender leaves. They can be eaten as salad greens, steamed, boiled, or used as a substitute for spinach. Some people think they taste like spinach, just like many folks say reptilian mystery meat "tastes just like chicken." Personally, I think lamb's quarter tastes more like something in the mustard family with a few leaves of Swiss chard thrown in the pot. The tender flowering tops, before the seeds begin to mature, are not unlike broccoli, and like broccoli are excellent raw, steamed, or boiled. Among those who graze the weed patches and wilderness areas, lamb's quarter is generally rated as one of the tastier "weeds" and is available from spring to the first hard frost in temperate regions.

The tender parts are easily stripped, or the flowering tops picked off, and eaten on the move. If you have time and a pot, they can be steamed or boiled. They are tasty and nutritious either way.

An annual, lamb's quarter self-seeds prolifically, and the bountiful seeds are very good as a potherb when green or as a grain when mature. Its sage-green, diamond-shaped leaves (often coated with a white powder on the underside) make it easy to identify. The shape of the leaves has given it a common nickname of "goose foot," although in some varieties the leaves are more spade-shaped when young or at the flowering top. Interestingly, another point of identification is that water will not wet the raw leaves. It commonly grows from a couple of feet to 5 feet tall in good conditions.

Above: Common, tasty, nutritious, lamb's quarters is a great trail food, common to meadows and river bottoms. Photo: Wikipedia.

Right: The flowering tops and seeds are edible as well. When mature, seeds are similar to the pseudocereal *C. quinoa* and are raised as a seed crop. Photo: Wikipedia.

Lamb's quarter is a substantial plant with a strong, fibrous stalk (which is not worth bothering with). Although the leaves are small compared to some vegetables, you get about a third of its green volume in cooked veggies. In some regions, this is one of many various plants called "pig weed." *A note of caution: just because a pig will eat a plant and thrive does not mean that it is safe for humans.*

AMARANTH
A Food and Weed the World Over

It's a safe bet the reader has seen amaranth, as its myriad species grow all over the world. *Almaranthus palmeri* (left), by far the most common in North America, was a crop raised by Native Americans for its greens and seeds. The only bad thing about amaranth, whichever variety, is that, like dandelion, it does so well it is invasive and gets no respect. It is raised all over the world as a seed crop; in

Amaranth grows the world over. It's a crop when raised on purpose, a weed when not. *A. retroflexus* is most common worldwide; *A. palmeri* (below) is most common in North America. Photos: Wikipedia.

the United States it is just cussed for its survivability—it has even developed a resistance for Roundup-type herbicides.

As food greens, amaranth tends to pick up and store excess soil nitrates, which can make it toxic to animals, and it contains oxalic acid (as do spinach and many other leafy greens), which in excess can contribute to kidney stones in humans. But as a trail food, a source of excellent grains, or a vegetable staple when it is cooked, it's hard to beat. When thoroughly dry, seeds may be hand-winnowed. Amaranth is another plant often called "pig weed," and a couple of the reasons it's such a survivor are its long taproot and all the (edible) seeds it produces. You will find amaranth cultivars in "alternative" seed catalogs, where it is promoted as a world-saving seed crop. It's more nutritious as a green than spinach or chard.

GRASS
No, Not My Favorite Either

I've already mentioned in passing that a lot of grasses are really good food sources. The best ones sometimes don't really *look* like grass (e.g., corn, cattails, bamboo, sugar cane), while some do, especially the "cereal" grasses, such as rice, wheat, and oats. And, conversely, there are many plants that may *look* like grass but are not and that are toxic, such as mountain wild iris. That's the bad news. The good news is, there are no recorded true grasses that are toxic. However, you do have to be very cautious of any grass seed heads that appear moldy or deformed or red and smutty, not brown and green colored: they may be infected with ergot or a similar fungal disease, which is highly poisonous.

Within these caveats, we need to look at grass as a food of last resort. Although there are thousands of species of grass, virtually all edible, *the main consideration is to be sure it is truly a grass*. The true grasses include cereals, bamboo, and the grasses of lawns (turf), and wild grassland or planted pastures. Grass has been grown as animal feed for roughly 6,000 years.

The second consideration for people food, aside from being sure you have a true grass, is that grass-eating animals have a digestive system that can handle the fibrous nature of grass, and humans do not. To be able to use fibrous grass or mostly husk seeds simply requires a gravel-filled gizzard or a multi-stomach/cud-chewing process to handle the fiber, which people do not have—no matter what a cavalier, desk-bound guru may write.

A common denominator among true grasses is that they have narrow, upward leaves and the seed head is borne on an upright stem

There is some kind of grass that will grow just about anywhere that any other plant will grow. Almost all grasses are at least partly edible. Photo: Wikipedia.

The seed head is a good identifier for true grasses, and a few have a seed head worth dealing with for food. This purple fountain grass, native to Africa, is now found all over as an invasive species. Photo: Wikipedia.

or branches. This stem may also have upright leaves branching from its lower part. Only the very tender, young grass leaves and shoots are edible, and at that stage (unless there happen to be identifiable mature specimens growing in juxtaposition, so you can make a positive identification of the young shoots), you risk grabbing something else, like a young iris shoot. A young grass shoot will be much more flexible than a comparable iris, yucca, or other shoot, and the inside white part will be tender, sweet, and crunchy. More mature grass may be chewed to extract the nutritional values and the indigestible fiber spit out.

The typical grass seed head is probably the best identifier, even though wild grasses will not have the luxurious seeds of our cereal crops (e.g., wheat, barley, oats). The best way to get at the tastiest part is to pull up on the green seed head, which separates the stem from a lower joint. The white, soft, and sweet inner butt of the stem is what you want. You won't get much off each one, but a million farm boys can't be wrong. Starving North Koreans, for instance, boil known-safe grass leaves and discard the inedible fiber. You can as well in a pinch. Or just chew it up, suck out the soluble/edible part, and spit out the inedible fiber.

Wild grass seed heads can also be smashed and boiled to extract any nutrition, or roasted and ground, but many are barely worth the effort. There is usually a lot more husk than grain, so much so that hand winnowing is impossible. Trying to swallow wild grass seed dry or to chew the seed head beard and all is an invitation to strangle.

There have been published allusions to wild grass seed that can be toxic unless cooked or roasted, but I have never been able to track down an actual reference. My own experience has been that few wild grass seeds will make a suitable on-the-move survival food, except for the wild "rice" that is sometimes marketed.

Wild rice is the premium wild grass seed, and if you are in its venue (mostly in the North-Central United States) when it is ripe and don't mind a little wading, it is well worth the effort. As far as taste, it is a quantum leap ahead of the traditional Asian strains of rice. It is generally harvested by being knocked into a container but, for personal use, can be hand-stripped.

WILD ASPARAGUS
The Springtime Treat

Wild asparagus is a good candidate for food on the go because it is hard to confuse with anything else, and, given a little water, it can be found almost anywhere there is neutral or alkaline soil. It's more rare in areas such as the West Coast that have predominantly acidic soil, but it thrives in virtually all temperature zones, even the Colorado Rockies at a mile high. It is also worthwhile looking for if you are in areas of abandoned farmsteads, as it can survive where the farm did not, even in the desert Southwest along stream banks.

A mature asparagus plant makes an airy, thin-leafed bush. When it dies down in the fall, it usually turns yellow and often stays light-colored through the winter. This color is the identifier for the tender spring shoots (inset). Photos: Wikipedia.

The edible part comprises the tender young shoots coming up from the perennial rootstalk, and the plants are most easily spotted by looking for the dead, branching plant from last year. What remains of last year's plants will depend on factors such as snow load, but they are generally cone-shaped and don't seem to turn dark like most other dead plants. If not broken down, the plants will run from 1–3 feet tall and will reflect a cone-shaped plant. There is no mistaking the tender young shoots at their base: they look like supermarket asparagus, but often thinner, and taste just the same—but better. They're fine raw but tastier cooked. Eat from the tip down to where it gets too fibrous for your taste. Examine carefully before you sample, as other plants will also send up an early shoot.

SALSIFY
"OYSTER PLANT"
Another Euro Import but Tasty

At one time a widely cultivated vegetable in Europe, the various varieties, and some hybrids, of salsify have made themselves at home on the North American continent, and at least one variety will be found in every state. The first one I saw appeared in my front lawn at 5,400 feet in Colorado.

Salsify is usually a biennial, sometimes an annual, and when it first sprouts it looks like a perfect rosette of crabgrass, with heavier, V-shaped leaves. It then sends up a branching, sage-colored stalk between 12 and 30 inches high, at the tips of which form pointed flower heads. These in turn develop purple or yellow flowers not unlike a dandelion. These flowers open early in the day but fold back

Salsify's typical yellow (sometimes purple) bloom, pollinated flower, and seed head. Photos: Wikipedia.

up about noon. Once pollinated, they fold back into a pointed cone and then form into a fluffy seed head like a dandelion's but much larger. At some point, all parts of this plant are edible, and the first-year root gives the plant its name "oyster plant," as it does indeed have a similar taste to fresh oysters. How big it is depends on soil and water conditions, but roots typically are up to an inch in diameter at the top and taper sharply to a point 8–10 inches below. All parts of the plant form latex.

First-year roots are very good; second-year roots are woody. New stalks are fine, and the tender flower buds before they bloom are good. It all may be eaten raw, but second-year roots may require the teeth of a woodchuck.

KUDZU
It's Here, Might as Well Eat It

Kudzu was introduced to North America at the Japanese pavilion in the 1876 Centennial Exposition in Philadelphia. It has a lot going for it: a perennial pea, it's a high-protein animal feed, has edible leaves and flowers, and produces excellent fiber in the vine and high-quality starch in the root. A legume, it fixes nitrogen and does well on poor soil. Franklin Delano Roosevelt's "we're from the government and we're here to help you" programs during the Depression planted hundreds of thousands of plants for erosion control. So far, so good. Now kudzu is spreading at the rate of 150,000 acres annually and overtaking every tree and building in its path like something out of a B movie. It is sometimes referred to, and not fondly, as "the plant that ate the South." Simply, it's just too much of a potentially good thing—but it's not all bad news, because you can eat it.

The tender young leaves can be eaten as greens raw or cooked; the flowers are also edible and can be dried for tea or boiled to make jelly. The edible starch in the root is extracted by simple leaching and straining and becomes "kudzu powder." The roots are fibrous, and if you select ones an inch or larger and chop them up as fine as you can and pound or macerate them in cold water rather like you would do with cattail roots, the starch dissolves. Next, you strain the root fiber out and let the liquid sit overnight; the starch settles out "like clay," and you pour off the water. My redneck kudzu advisor said there is a good market for this product if you redissolve and strain it until you have a fine consistency. But they just use it in its rough, gray state to add to soups and stews, and their palates are about as enthused over it as they are about trading their BBQ for tofu.

There is a lot to like about kudzu; that's why we were seduced into planting it all over the South. It now smothers trees and buildings at 150,000 acres a year. A perennial legume, it has a pretty and edible flower (inset). Photos: Wikipedia.

But for eating on the go in the spring and summer, the tender young leaves and flowers will feed you, and in the winter months the roots can be a life-saving source of wholesome carbs.

WILD CARROT
Look for the Hairy Stems

Daucus carota (common North American names include wild carrot or Queen Anne's lace) is native to the temperate regions of Europe and southwest Asia, and it has become naturalized in North America and Australia, where it is usually considered a noxious weed. Domesticated carrots are cultivars of a subspecies, *Daucus carota* subsp. *sativus.*

Like all carrots, the wild carrot is a biennial plant, usually flowering and bearing seeds in its second year. Depending on soil conditions, it typically grows 3–4 feet tall in the second year and flowers from June to August. The umbels (flower heads) are off-white or pale pink before they open and then bright white and rounded when in full flower, measuring 1.5 to 3 inches across. As they mature, they cup upward. When they turn to seed, they contract and become concave like a bird's nest, and when dry the umbel breaks off and blows in the wind. Individual seeds tend to stick to clothing and fur.

Similar in appearance to the deadly poison hemlock, wild carrot is distinguished by the size of its umbels, fine hairs on its stems and leaves, a root that smells strongly like carrots, and usually a single dark-red flower in the center of the round flower clump.

Mature (second-year) roots are terribly woody, although they can be pounded and boiled and the fiber discarded. Flowering specimens are most useful to locate a patch of wild carrots, so you can dig the tender first-year roots. They are small and white, and have a strong carrot flavor. Note that some people get a topical allergic reaction to wild carrot leaves and stems.

Wild carrot flowers are presented in a symmetrical round arrangement, with the center flower usually being deep red. As the flower matures, it cups upward. Its typical environs are pasturelands and hedgerows. Photo: Wikipedia.

Important: Poison hemlock, as was used in early Greek times to kill Socrates, is also now found in North America as an invasive weed. Note that the individual leaves look more like parsley, whereas wild carrot leaves are more feathery and look like the carrot that they are. The flowers of the hemlock are presented as smaller clumps and do not have the red center of the wild carrot. Hemlock leaves and stems do not have fine hairs, as does the wild carrot. Hemlock grows in wet soil, in damp pastures, and along ditches. Wild carrot prefers typical pasture-type lands. And wild carrot leaves and roots have a strong carrot smell. Some people get an allergic reaction to wild carrot leaves. Photo: Wikipedia.

PLANTAIN
The Herb, Not the Banana

Plantain, especially *Plantago major*, has hitchhiked across the globe from its native Europe. The related *P. lanceolata* (right), aka "ribwort," grows right alongside the broader-leaved *P. major*. There are even cultivars of this perennial herb. However, it is also a medicinal herb and pretty tough chewing unless you find really young shoots. Its flavor is OK; on a 1–10 scale about a 3 to my palate.

If you take blood thinners, avoid this herb. If not, then maybe it

The plantain was one of the first European weeds inadvertently introduced to North America. Photos: Wikipedia.

will help get you home. There are other varieties, all of which have the flowers and seeds on an upright central stalk. When completely mature and very dry, the seeds are easily stripped by hand, threshed between the hands, and the chaff blown away. The seeds are usually mentioned as edible but have a laxative effect. We boiled them up as a grain when we were kids but noticed no laxative effect. If they do affect you in that fashion, the boiled leaves are a common folk remedy for diarrhea.

WILD VIOLET
And Some Are Yellow

This doesn't need much description, because everybody knows what a violet looks like. However, wild violets, native to North America, will include the white Canadian wild violet, pictured below, that is native to the eastern part of the continent, and the bright yellow "Johnny-jump-up" common to the Western part of the continent. There are some 400 kinds of *violas*, to include the pansies and the "viola" cross between violets and pansies, and all are edible. The yellow or white wild ones do not have the characteristic sweet violet scent, but all their flowers and heart-shaped leaves are edible. Both are best when young and tender. If you find yourself where man has lived before, you may also find scented cultivars that have gone feral.

Wild violet—it's what's for dinner. Photo: Wikipedia.

ICE PLANT
A Succulent Succulent

There are many nonrelated plants called "ice plant," but here I refer to the South African native *Carpobrotus edulis,* which is now found in most frostfree coastal regions of the United States, where it has been planted for erosion control and often has taken over, spreading with man's help all the way to Baja. The good news is, it is edible. So is its tart, fig-like fruit. The fruit is eaten raw or made into preserves; the juicy, pulpy leaves can be eaten raw.

The *Carpobrotus edulis* you are likely to find in North America

Ice plant will be familiar to any GI who ever served at a warm-climate base with an erosion problem. Uncounted acres, especially in coastal areas, have been planted with this adaptable, self-seeding plant. Photo: Wikipedia.

is a creeping, mat-forming succulent species and member of the stone plant family *Aizoaceae*, one of about 30 species in the genus *Carpobrotus*. It has a close relative *Carpobrotus chilensis* (sea fig), which is smaller and less aggressive, and the two species hybridize readily throughout their ranges in California. The large 2.5–6 inch diameter flowers of *C. edulis* are yellow or light pink, whereas the smaller, 1.5–2.5 inch diameter *C. chilensis* flowers are deep magenta.

The plants and fruit are eaten by most herbivores, and as they only grow in frostfree areas, they grow year round, at the rate of about 3 feet a year, to a diameter of 170 feet, and they bloom nearly year round. Ice plant foliage can turn a vibrant red to yellow if stressed by drought or cold.

PRICKLY LETTUCE
The Wild Side of Side Salads

This hardy and prolific weed can be found on every continent, and everywhere it has been found it has been eaten. It is the closest relative to the varieties of lettuce cultivars you see in the store, but in comparison it is not at all succulent.

Prickly lettuce is an annual or biennial, with a slightly animal smell. A prolific producer of small yellow flowers and airborne seeds, it can be found anywhere as a weed, especially in plowed ground. It grows from a central smooth stalk, and the leaves look like a sage-colored, long oak leaf. The way that the base of the leaf wraps around the stalk is an identifier. The back of the leaf has spines along the white central vein. The leaves and stalk contain bitter latex, which has soporific qualities if eaten in quantity, because of the opiates it contains. It is also a mild diuretic.

Prickly lettuce grows from 1 to 4 feet tall, depending on its environs, and flowers at the top. The smaller, newer leaves have the best flavor and texture. Because of the bitter sap, it is best cooked. The spines on the back of the mature leaves should be rubbed off if they are going to be used in a salad or when grazing.

Looking not unlike a domesticated small-leaf lettuce that has gone to seed, the wild prickly lettuce has a stronger flavor and provides more nutrition. Photo: Wikipedia.

WILD ONIONS
They All Smell Like Onions

Domestic onions and garlic are in the allium family, and various members of the family grow wild as native or invasive species all over North America. All are edible if cooked; the milder-flavored ones are good raw. All are distinguished by the onion/garlic smell and taste, and some wild varieties are unpleasantly strong.

All have the typical allium flower head atop a slender stalk. As most have very slender leaves, they are often easiest to spot by the flower head or by the odor when you are walking through grassy meadows. Flowers are typically pink to purple to blue. Various native allium grow in many elevations and settings. Perhaps the best is the wild leek locally known as "ramps" in Appalachia, which is easier to spot and harvest, and is a very tasty part of local cuisine, tasting not unlike green onions with a twinge of garlic. Ramps are excellent with pork.

(Clockwise from top left) Pacific mountain onion, twincrest onion, "ramp" (wild leek), and crow garlic. Photos: Wikipedia.

THISTLES
Poor Man's Artichokes

Many herbaceous plants with stickers are called "thistles," but many are not really thistles. Here we'll refer to the genus *Cirsium*. The ones of interest to us as food have purple flowers: the roots and flowers are edible raw or boiled or steamed. Young stalks can be (carefully) peeled and boiled or steamed. Fine stickers can be quickly singed off in a fire before peeling. Most thistle roots are sweet. Both thistles shown here are naturalized, invasive weeds from Europe. Compared to eating the globe artichoke (a cousin), eating thistle flowers is a little fiddly: on the move, you can hold the flower by the purple petals, use a sharp knife to cut the stem, and then cut away the sticker-covered sheath.

There are many thistles native to or naturalized in North America. The roots and flowers of those with lavender-blue petals are edible, usually sweet. Left is creeping thistle (aka, "Canadian" thistle); bull thistle (aka, "Scotch" thistle) is at right. Photos: Wikipedia.

COMMON BURDOCK
The Edible Hitchhiker

Arctium minus, commonly known as common burdock, is a biennial thistle. Native to Europe, it has hitchhiked all over the world via the hooked barbs on the mature flower pods—which inspired the Swiss inventor of Velcro, George de Mestral, in 1948. Anyone in North America who has raised long-haired farm dogs has met burdock.

Common burdock and its cousin, greater burdock, are biennials. The edible parts are the first-year root and the tender young leaves, if you can stand the bitterness, or the young stalks, which must be peeled. For our purposes here, look for young stalks to peel. Even tender young leaves are so bitter to my taste as to be nearly emetic, and the roots, the parts for which they are raised in Asia, grow too

A quintessential hitchhiker, burdock is identified by its Velcro-like seed heads.
Photo: Wikipedia.

deep to be easily harvested unless you have serious digging tools and time. Leaves are long and oval-shaped, bottom leaves more angular with wavy edges; all leaves are dark green above and hairy. The best identifier is the Velcro-like seed head, the plant blossoming from July–October with a pink-to-purple flower like a thistle. Second-year roots are also edible but very fibrous: boil them, chew out the starch, and spit out the fiber, if you have time.

DOCK
Only for Survival

Rumex obtusifolius, usually known as broad-leaved dock, is a perennial weed native to Europe but can now be found in North America and other countries. It comes in several varieties, all marginally edible, and I have found *R. obtusifolius* more common in the Far West. It is characterized by typically red stems and a coarser leaf than *R. crispus* (below left). As kids we called it "Indian tobacco," and, of course, it is neither Indian nor tobacco. It rather looks like a woody dwarf rhubarb or a woody beetroot that has bolted.

All kinds of dock can be used as a wild leaf vegetable; before

The red-veined *obtusifolius*. All dock varieties are edible, but few are tasty. Use tender young leaves, boil well, and change the water a few times. Photos: Wikipedia.

they have unfurled, the young leaves should be boiled in several changes of water to remove as much of the oxalic acid in the leaves as possible. They are also edible when young and tender as a grab-and-go food, if you can find nothing better. Some people think of this as a staple food, and some species were at one time a cultivar, but I would guess the big fans of dock as a staple have not yet passed a kidney stone. All vegetables high in oxalic acid contribute to the formation of calcium oxalate dihydrate kidney stones. Personally, I'm saving my kidneys for rhubarb and spinach, both of which I truly enjoy. There is a big difference in taste among species and how young the leaves are, but any can help get you home if that's all there is.

WATER LILIES
These Are *Not* Lotuses
and May Be Inedible

There are some 70 varieties of water lily around the world, including many native to North America and probably an equal number that have been brought here. Some have edible parts. For instance, the seeds of the yellow-flowered water lily native to Klamath Lake in southern Oregon were harvested in great quantity by the Indians and stored for winter use as well. They primarily just roasted them and, according to a USDA paper ca. 1897, ate them liked popcorn. Early 1700 writings by an English author reported that Native Americans in "New England" boiled "water lily" roots

These are water lilies on a lake in Canada. Note the slot (sinus) from the edge of the leaf to the stem and that the pads float on the water and do not extend above the surface on the stem. These traits are common to all North American water lilies. If somebody tells you they are good to eat, they may be. But say, "Sure, you first!" Photo: Wikipedia.

for a long time and that they had a taste like "sheep's liver." The problem with that report, however, is that in British writings of the time, water lily and lotus were both called "water lily," and as the paper was not illustrated, we don't know which he referenced.

Various mammals eat various parts of various water lilies. But unless all mammals can eat all parts of all water lilies, they are not an appropriate inclusion for this book, as the purpose of this work is to feed you to get home, not poison you with bad, second-sourced advice. You will find water lily roots and tubers listed as edible in otherwise credible field guides, but like the cavalier expert who gives you his favorite recipe for bracken fern, you may not want to trust them until you have tried it on Mikey.

AMERICAN LOTUS
This Is the *Real* McCoy

Currently recognized under the botanical name *Nelumbo lutea*, American lotus is a native of the American Southeast and parts of Central America. It was apparently relocated north by Native Americans who carried it as food as far north as Minnesota and Massachusetts. The largest native wild flower in North America, it has 7–11 inch off-white or pale yellow blossoms, each with a couple of dozen pointed petals, blooming from late spring to fall, depending on location.

It grows in lakes and swamps or areas subject to flooding that have a high water table. The roots are anchored in the mud, but the leaves and flowers emerge above the water's surface: The leaves may be below water if the water rises, or they may sit up to 6 feet above the water, but they do not always float on the water as does a water lily. The large, round, pulpy leaves have their stem located dead center, reminding me of a giant miner's lettuce (see page 123). The lotus has no slit from the edge of the leaf to the stem, as on a water lily. The leaves typically are from 12 to 18 inches in diameter, with larger ones assuming a slight funnel shape, probably for structural reasons. Mature plants range from 1 to 5 feet tall. Although native, it is sometimes considered a weed if man wants to use a particular body of water for another purpose.

Although the premise of this book is that the reader may already be cold and wet, if your situation is such that you can do a little shallow free diving, the American lotus has large, edible, banana-shaped tubers that grow at the end of the rhizomes, a few inches below the mud. They can be peeled, sliced, and boiled; sliced and dried for later use; or baked like a potato. They have an interesting pattern of

The largest wild flower in the business (top left), American lotus is identified by its large, round leaf with the stem in the middle (top right); the strange-looking seed heads (above) have a nut behind every hole. Photos: Wikipedia.

longitudinal holes that run the length of the tuber. Tender shoots and leaves are edible but even after a couple changes of water do not taste very good to me.

Note the first and third photos on the previous page. The interesting perforated disc in the middle of the flower develops into a large 6-inch seedpod that looks like some sort of strange marine life or the distributor cap for an exotic engine. The immature seeds form behind the holes, and they are edible raw or boiled. The mature seeds, large and brown (go for the plump ones that fill the holes), can be roasted and eaten as nuts or ground into flour: extract them, pierce with a knife blade, and roast. The meat splits in two, kind of like a peanut, and if it has a bitter green sprout, remove it. Dried whole, the nuts are indestructible. They are very hard to crack, and some lotus seeds can remain viable for more than a thousand years. But if shucked when tender and then dried, they keep for a long time and, like any dried nut, make good trail food. One further advantage of the nut as opposed to the tuber is that if you are there the right time of year, when the water is lower in the fall, odds are in your favor to collect them from around the edges without even getting wet.

Hybrid cultivars are on the market, as well.

BLACK WALNUTS
Everybody Loves a Nut

Throughout man's history, it's probably a safe bet that we have eaten more acorns than any other sort of tree nut, just because oak trees are ubiquitous and can be very big and very productive. Can you imagine, for instance, a filbert tree that is 4 feet at the butt, 100 feet tall, and produces for a hundred years? Once cultivars of other nuts were developed, nuts that were edible with no leaching or fussing, the oak largely fell out of favor. However, it's still a toss-up which is less work, leaching an acorn or trying to get the meat out of a black walnut with a rock. There are several nuts native to North America, and they are all tasty and nutritious—and being high in calories, they are a good fuel.

There are a few related black walnut trees native to North America: the Eastern black walnut, the smaller Texas black walnut, and what I assume are subspecies of these two, such as the scruffy little ones growing in the Arizona desert. They will cross. Black walnut is native from southern Ontario, west to South Dakota, south to Florida, and southwest to central Texas but is found all over as isolated natives and as transient natives or man-planted escapees. I have even found what appeared to be native stands of the Texas black walnut growing straight and tall in the Bradshaw Mountains of northern Arizona, at 5,000 feet and subject to seriously cold winters. Although they grow best in temperate regions, they are hardy; for that reason, black walnut root stock is used the world over to graft English walnuts.

The nuts grow in a thick, green husk that turns yellow and is readily removed when they are ripe. The husk has a strong iodine smell and will stain your hands brown. They can be dumped in a

An American native, black walnut now grows all over the world—wild, planted, or as rootstock for grafting. Photo: Wikipedia.

pond to stun fish. At home, the nuts are husked and then dried. In the woods you could dry them by fire if you have time. They take a little work to crack but come apart best if you pound them on the pointed end—whack them a few times with a rock to blunt the point, smash hard to knock them apart, and then use a small stick or knife point to remove the very tasty meat.

BUTTERNUT
Well Named and Delicious

Butternut is a native species of walnut, sometimes called a "white walnut," originally found in the eastern United States and southeast Canada from New Brunswick and southern Quebec west to Minnesota, south to Alabama, and southwest to northern Arkansas. They have been planted all over as a desirable nut and for lumber. I saw my first ones as a kid in Okanogan country in northern Washington.

Butternut bark is a light gray, and the leaves are yellow-tinted all season, making it easy to spot from a distance. It tends to grow straighter than a black walnut. It favors stream banks and well-drained soils where it can get sunlight. It does not compete in deep woods. The nuts are in bunches of two to six. The nut looks very much like a black walnut but is lemon shaped. It also has a green husk, which tends to turn brown and rot but not come off as cleanly as that of the black walnut. It matures in midfall.

Once the mature nut falls from the tree, if the husk is not removed it dries to a leathery consistency that is a real chore to remove. I think the nuts are the hardest to open of any native American nut, but they are worth it. You probably will not be able to crack them with a log, so look for suitable rocks. If you whack them just right on the point of the fault line so the halves separate, the meat is easy to extract.

If you think you found an upright-growing black walnut and the fruit is shaped like this, you have a butternut. Lucky you—it may be the tastiest nut there is. Photo: Wikipedia.

WILD FILBERTS (HAZELNUT)
The Easiest to Open

Hazelnuts are probably the easiest wild nut to open, and they are tasty. The downside is, some folks are bothered by the fuzzies on the outer husk, and it has been my experience that if you are going to compete with the local rodents, you have to pick them while they are still green, whereas cultivars are left to ripen on the tree and shaken off. If you have time, you can roast the green nuts husk and all in the fire, which removes the fuzzies and the husk and "ripens" the nut. In their green state, immature nuts have a milky juice and an almost coconutty flavor.

Wild hazelnuts also tend to be large, suckering shrubs, one growing here and one there. There are at least two native North American hazelnuts, and in southern Washington State they have found fossilized specimens of a third. They will cross with cultivars, and they're all good. The fuzzy, strong, rounded leaves are a favorite toilet paper substitute for woods-roaming kids in the Northwest.

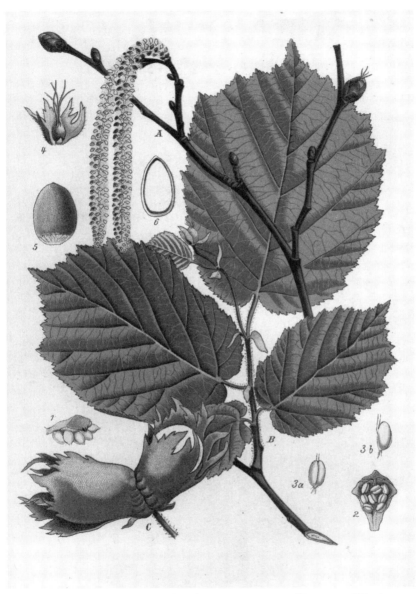

This tasty nut may be found anywhere in temperate zones of Europe and North America, and although different varieties grow differently, the leaves and nuts are very similar. Photo: Wikipedia.

SHAGBARK HICKORY
The Best Hickory Nut

In the same family as the walnut and related to the pecan, not all wild hickory nuts are created equal. Only the ones from the shagbark hickory (there is a northern and a southern variety) are considered fit for human consumption. Others are too bitter for people food but are eaten by wildlife. Mature trees are identified by the characteristic shaggy bark, not always evident on younger trees. The taste of wild hickory nuts reminds some folks of Grape-Nuts.

The edible variety of wild hickory nuts comes from the shagbark hickory tree, obviously well named. Inset: The hickory nut grows in a thick husk that falls away when mature. Main photo: Texas A & M University; inset photo: Wikipedia.

WILD PECAN
A Natural Wonder

If you're living off the woods in the south-central United States, it doesn't get any better than pecans. Native Americans long harvested and traded pecans, which are a relative of the hickory. All pecan varieties are delicious and have a thin, easily broken shell. They grow in a thick husk like a hickory, but when mature, the husk falls away and the pecans drop to the ground.

The pecan tree often grows to more than 100 feet tall, spreads to 70 feet, and can have a 4-foot-diameter trunk. A mature tree can bear nuts for more than 300 years. Oddly, pecans did not really become a popular cultivar—perhaps because of the natural bounty—until after the American Civil War, and now it is grown worldwide in temperate zones. Some 400 million pounds of pecans are produced annually from some 10 million cultivated pecan trees in the United States, about 90 percent of the world crop. This does not count those that fall in the woods: those are for you.

The pecan tree grows to a large size, like this specimen in Abilene, Texas; bears for hundreds of years; and (left) produces excellent quality nuts that are easy to open and have been harvested since aboriginal times. Photo: Wikipedia.

WILD ROSES
A Rose Is a Rose Is a Treat

Native wild roses and derelict domestic roses can be found all over North America's temperate regions. Most domestic roses are grafted onto a wild root for its hardiness, so surviving hybrid domestic roses are far less common, but there is more than one variety of wild rose. In season, the flower petals are edible and tasty but not very substantial. The berries, called rose hips, are edible, and one great attraction to rose hips is that they will often be found hanging on the long, naked canes poking out of the winter snow. They taste rather like apricots and are exceptionally high in vitamin C, which may be just what you need in the dead of winter.

Some papers state that rose seeds are toxic, containing cyanogens that can convert to cyanide. If birds eat them, I do not know if this is true, as birds are especially sensitive to cyanide because of their high metabolism. However, the fuzzy hairs surrounding the seeds can be extremely irritating, and you should avoid handling them. These hairs certainly should not be eaten. Mean little kids routinely use them for itching powder (or at least they used to), and they cause considerable irritation of the mouth and intestinal tract if eaten.

To avoid them, if the fruit is quite ripe and not dry, pick it by grabbing it with the thumb and fingers, pinching, and pulling it straight off. The outer sheath and most of the meat usually pulls off, leaving the inner part with the seeds and hairs on the bush. With immature rose hips, pick the fruit, split it with a knife, and then use the knifepoint to remove the entire inside portion with the seeds and hairs. Be sure to get it all. Rose hips are such good nutrition that they are worth the hassle.

Most roses found in the wild will have single petals in either pink or white. Wild blooms are usually about 1 1/2 inches across. Many have no aroma, but rose petals are edible. Photo: Wikipedia.

Rose hips, the berry of the rose bush, have a very high vitamin C content. Avoid the seeds, especially the fuzz around the seeds, in the inner portion. Photo: Wikipedia.

Rose hips are traditionally mashed and boiled for the juice, the irritating fuzz filtered out, and the juice further reduced to syrup. But when you find ripe fruit that will pull off cleanly, they make a great tonic on the move. Also, when they are plentiful and you have some to waste, the outside good part may be simply pared off with a knife and eaten. They vary greatly in size, from the size of a pea to the size of a very large olive.

BEARBERRY
Food in the Far North

In season, wild fruits and berries can provide good grazing, and even after their optimum season some will dry on the plant and provide later food for wildlife—or you, if you get there first. Not all fruits, however, are edible by man. I'll give a brief overview in the following sections of what is common to North America that is good fare, many of which the reader will recognize from its having been domesticated. A botanist will note that many fruits called berries are not berries, and some items we call vegetables are actually berries,

Bearberry—favored by bears, tolerated by hungry humans. Photo: Wikipedia.

Eating on the Run

e.g., tomatoes, pumpkin, and watermelon. But for foraging we'll lump them all together and leave it at that, unless you want study further, so you can win friendly wagers that the 1,200-pound Atlantic Giant pumpkin is really a berry.

Bearberries are three species of dwarf shrubs in the genus *Arctostaphylos*. Unlike the other species of *Arctostaphylos* (like manzanita), they are adapted to arctic and subarctic climates of northern North America, Asia, and Europe. Bearberry (common bearberry: *Arctostaphylos uva-ursi*) is a low-growing, woody groundcover shrub a few inches high. The leaves are evergreen, shiny, and small, and feel thick and stiff. The underside of the leaves is lighter green. New stems can be red if the plant is in full sun but are green in shadier areas. Older stems are brown. In spring, they have white or pink flowers. The fruit is a red berry, which bears make good use of, and is edible for humans, although not particularly tasty. On the plus side, bearberry does grow in cold regions or at altitudes few other plants can.

CRANBERRY
Good for Turkeys or Travelers

Introduced to the Pilgrims by friendly natives, the first cranberries were being farmed in North America by 1816. Native to the Northeast, they are now grown in several states, including Oregon and Washington. The cranberry is a low-growing shrub with thin, trailing branches, which will be found native in acidic bogs and sphagnum moss beds. The flowers are pink, and the berries come on as white, at which time they are edible and then continue to mature to pink and maroon in late fall. Aside from habitat and appearance, the tart-bitter but pleasing taste is the best identifier.

Traditional for holiday dinners and especially good with fowl and pork, cranberries are also a prime forage food in late fall. Photo: Wikipedia.

ELDERBERRIES
Easy to Pick but Variable in Taste

Elderberries can produce a prodigious amount of easily harvested fruit, but some are so tart that they are used mostly for cooking, preserves, and winemaking. Some stink when raw. Even the blue varieties, mostly found in the West, are best when cooked, as the raw berries make some people nauseated. This appears to vary with individuals and with varieties, and it may even be because they are so readily harvested and have a low pH that overeating may contribute to stomach distress. In any case, cooking improves the flavor.

Only the flowers and berries are edible; the flowers make an excellent tea or at home can be steamed, mashed, and fried like a

Dark- or powder-blue elderberries grow on a tall, woody bush that has a pithy center and produces easily harvested berries. The berries are very tart to eat but are used for jams, jellies, wine, or survival food. Photo: Wikipedia.

fritter. The berries are small and a bit seedy, but they grow in big bunches, are easy to pick, and make decent preserves. The red elderberry, more common in some areas of the West Coast, is a different deal of the cards: West Coast natives would harvest them, cook them by steaming, and dry them in thin loaves for possible hard times, when they would mix them with more palatable fruit. However, raw red berries make almost everybody nauseous, and the foliage is reported as downright toxic. I find the red fruit, even cooked, disgusting. But if it's all you have, and you can cook it, go for it—or keep looking for the blue ones, as they share venues.

Although both flowers and fruit are edible, all elderberry fruit *must be ripe* to be edible. The large, woody stems have a soft pith center that is easily removed, making them a favorite item for kid projects but not for anything involving food.

CROWBERRIES
Better Than the Name Implies

Crowberries are a pleasant treat, one of few found on the subarctic tundra and muskeg. It is a staple among the Inuit and Sami people, who often mix it with fat or with other berries. Of particular interest for one traveling in a survival mode is that the berries stay on the bush and do not spoil, often until new growth starts the next spring, which greatly extends their window of availability.

Crowberries will stay on the bush until picked or spring growth starts. Photo: Wikipedia

AUTUMNBERRY "AUTUMN-OLIVE"

An Invasive Import That Is Useful

Elaeagnus umbellata is an import from Asia and is also called Japanese silverberry because the berries are silver when they first appear and, even when deep red and ripe, retain tiny silver or brown spots. The new spring leaves also have a silvery sheen, which turns to deep green as the summer progresses. The spring flowers have a heavy, sweet scent.

This hardy shrub grows into a small tree up to 16 feet tall and was originally brought here because it can tolerate very barren soil, being one of the few non-legumes that can fix atmospheric nitrogen in the soil for itself. In theory this would be good for surrounding plants, but the autumnberry is wont to choke out anything in the area, which works out well for its plan to become the preeminent invasive shrub. It has been successful in its intended role for reclaiming barren ground, such as mine tailings and erosion-prone, disturbed hillsides, but it has become a pest where it was not intended to go, choking out native species. But it's not all bad news: the berries, ripe in the fall, are palatable if a little tart, usually very abundant, and nutritious: they contain several times more of the antioxidant lycopene than even tomatoes have.

The crown of the bush tends to be a little pokey, but that is not a problem because even low branches bear heavy loads of fruit. They attract bugs, but aside from that they are a good fruit to graze on the run. Back at the ranch, they make good pies and preserves, and once seeded they dry well into fruit strips. Unripe fruits are very tart and unpalatable; the soft, ripe berries readily come off in your hand. If you like the ease with which you can get quantities of elderberries,

An interloper that at least contributes, although it has proven invasive, the autumn-berry is good at erosion control and provides a great deal of tasty fruit for man and beast. Photo: Wikipedia.

you'll love autumnberries, as they are a prodigious producer. The leathery seeds are not toxic, but unless you are bored and need something to do, you can just spit them out.

RUSSIAN OLIVE
Barely Russian, Not an Olive

Originating in Western Asia, the Russian olive is one of the most invasive large shrubs/small trees ever introduced into the United States. The *Elaeagnus angustifolia* is a close relative to the equally invasive autumnberry (page 96) and shares its ability to fix nitrogen and grow in otherwise barren mineral soil. It is not at all related to the olive, its name just springing from the fact that the silver-sage-colored leaves look rather like an olive, the tree is generally shaped like many olive trees, and the fruit, a seeded drupe, bears a superficial resemblance to an olive when green.

The fruit is usually about 1/2 inch long by 3/8 inch in diameter and has a rather thin layer of sweet, mealy pulp. The pulp is dry, reminding me somewhat of a dried date, and is slightly astringent. If you have pliers you can liberate the seed inside the pit, which is quite tasty but not very big. In a good year these small trees will be loaded; birds like them and have seeded them all over the arid West, which although an invasive species can be a blessing where there is nothing else edible. The drupes come on green and ripen to yellowish-tan or redwood-colored fruit.

Because they are now all over the West, they comprise a valuable source of ad hoc groceries in season, especially in areas where nothing else grows. The bird-seeded new plants will bloom and bear in only three years. The tree has serious thorns, but fortunately not a lot of them and they do not interfere with picking the fruit. It was originally introduced as an ornamental and for erosion control. One grows outside my bedroom window, tolerated because of the scent when they bloom. Small birds eat the pulp of the fruit; squirrels eat the nut

Like that of many other invasive plants, the edible fruit of the Russian olive might as well be eaten, since it's here. Photo: Wikipedia.

of the seed and spit the hulls in my eaves trough. It makes good fire-wood and turns well on a lathe, looking similar to genuine olive.

WILD GRAPE
Every Region Has Its Favorite

There are a number of wild grapes native to North America. They range from white to dark blue andfrom large to small, but not all are truly edible. The mustang wild grape native to Texas is so acidic most folks have to wear rubber gloves to pick them and then treat them before they can be used. Taste grapes first, and remember that grapes often will leave lots of raisins dried on the vine that you can take with you. Many excellent cultivars were developed from native American grapes, such as the Concord (blue) and Niagara (white).

This *Vitis californica* is typical of native North American wild grapes. Photo: Wikipedia.

OREGON GRAPE
Oregon, Yes; Grape, No

Oregon "grape" grows all over the West, in small bush and larger shrub varieties. It is one of the earliest to bloom, with small, bright-yellow flowers, and it bears clusters of 1/4-inch, powdery-blue fruit that look like miniature Concord grapes. It has holly-shaped, prickly evergreen leaves, many of which will be red, making it an easy bush to spot in the deep woods. Grown as a decorative shrub and often gathered for floral arrangements, it is bird-seeded so may be found anywhere. The berries are very flavorful but very tart and have a large seed. Because of their tartness, they were often mixed with sweeter fruits by native peoples. They make great jelly. The root makes yellow dye; the berries make blue dye. Properly called *Mahonia aquifolium, Berberidaceae* is related to the barberry.

The state flower of Oregon, Oregon grape is a tart treat in season. Photo: Wikipedia.

PERSIMMON
Good *When Ripe*

If you find a persimmon tree and the fruit is dead ripe, you are in for a treat. If it's not dead ripe, then not so much. The American persimmon (*Diospyros virginiana*) is native to the eastern United States and is higher in vitamin C and calcium than the Japanese persimmon.

Persimmons range from New England to Florida, and west to Texas, Louisiana, Oklahoma, and Kansas. The tree grows wild but has been cultivated for its fruit and wood since prehistoric times by Native Americans. It grows to more than 60 feet in well-drained soil. The fruit is round or oval and usually orange-yellow, ranging to bluish in color and from about an inch to 2 1/2 inches in diameter. When dead ripe and soft in the fall, they are very sweet; anything less and they are astringently sour from the tannin they contain.

American persimmons come on late in the fall, and the leaves have often fallen before the fruit falls. The fruit must be dead ripe and soft to be edible. Photos: Wikipedia.

SALAL
Mild and Sweet and Common

Salal is native to the American Northwest from Alaska to central California but was introduced to England and has adapted so well there it is considered an invasive weed. In areas with adequate rainfall it forms nearly impenetrable thickets. An evergreen, it is harvested for floral arrangements and grown as an ornamental shrub.

It has small pink flowers that are slightly sticky and produces quantities of small, dark-blue to purple fruit, which looks like berries but is actually a swollen sepal. They are easily harvested, mild flavored, sweet, and a little seedy. It was a staple among hunter-gather peoples of the West Coast, dried for winter use or as a component of foods such as pemmican. It is a great grab-and-go food, one of the best offerings in low coastal areas with deep woods.

The shiny evergreen leaves make salal easy to identify, and (inset) these sticky pink flowers develop into soft, dark-blue fruit, readily harvested. Photos: Wikipedia.

CHOKECHERRY
Well Named but Nutritious

The chokecherry, *Prunus virginiana*, is well named. Although entirely edible and one of the most important fruits in the diet of many Native American tribes of the Northern Rockies, Northern Plains, and boreal forest region of Canada and the United States, chokecherries take some getting used to.

The brushy, suckery trees have typical reddish-brown, smooth cherry-tree bark; are usually small; and often grow in thickets. The fruit reminds me of a tart pie cherry, except there is less fruit on the pit, and unless you only pick the dark, dead-ripe fruit, they are too sour to be enjoyable. Many sources cite the unripe fruit and pits, and leaves of the chokecherry as toxic. They do dry well and were often mixed with sweeter fruits. At home they make excellent preserves and tolerable pies, although they are a chore to pit (use a small soda straw).

A nutritious and staple fruit of many northern Native American tribes, chokecherries are tart even when dead ripe. Photo: Wikipedia.

GROUND CHERRY ("CAPE GOOSEBERRY")
Lunch in a Lantern

Native to North America, this plant, usually a self-seeding annual, is neither a cherry nor a gooseberry, nor does it have anything to do with the Cape of South Africa. Related to the tomato, it has many cultivars available and, as feral cultivars or native plants, may be found almost anywhere except regions with late freezes or extremely dry conditions. In favorable areas, these plants grow prolifically and self-seed indefinitely.

Ground cherries are very sweet, with a citrus-tomato flavor. They may be eaten right off the plant if dead ripe, dried, or used for preserves. The marble-sized natives, with yellow-orange fruits, develop in a "Chinese lantern" husk ("cape") that turns brown and splits open when ripe. Green fruits and leaves are toxic: only eat ripe, soft fruit.

The "cape gooseberry," or ground cherry, is native to North America and is related to the tomatillo popular in Tex-Mex cuisine but sweeter. Photos: Wikipedia.

SERVICEBERRY
Many Variations on a Theme

The serviceberry, properly known as *Amelanchier*, from whichever species and by whatever name, can provide excellent early-summer grazing. In the rose family, it is regionally known as shadbush, shadwood, or shadblow; serviceberry or sarvisberry; wild pear; Juneberry; saskatoon; sugarplum or wild plum; and chuckley pear. Serviceberry not only has a confusing array of local names, it comes in a confusing array of varieties—but they're all good. It comprises a genus of about 20 species of deciduous-leaved shrubs and small trees in the rose family, which can also hybridize locally.

Various species grow from a foot to 60 feet tall—some are small trees; some are multistemmed, clump-forming shrubs; and even others form extensive low, shrubby patches. The bark is gray or less often brown, and in tree species smooth or fissuring when older. The leaves are deciduous, often with the appearance of small, rounded apple leaves.

The flowers appear in early spring, typically white. The fruit is a berry-like pome, red to purple to nearly black at maturity, varying with species from a quarter-inch to about an inch in diameter. Maturing in summer, the fruits vary from insipidly mild to very sweet. A typical fruit, the Saskatoon berry, is shown here as representative. Serviceberry is an important wild food source for man and beast.

One or more varieties of serviceberry are native to every state but Hawaii, and they vary from small bushes to some 60 feet tall. This Saskatoon berry, for which the Canadian city was named, is typical. This species is also raised commercially. Photo: Wikipedia.

SALMONBERRY
The Least of the Raspberries

Salmonberries are related to blackberries and raspberries, and grow very much like a large orange raspberry. They are native to the west coast of North America from west-central Alaska to California.

They grow like a typical "cane" berry but can reach 12 feet in height. They bloom in early spring with a purple, five-pointed flower, and the fruit ripens late summer to early fall. The fruit is not at all unpleasant, but I find it watery in flavor and texture. The fruit is orange and very much looks like salmon roe or a large orange raspberry.

In Oregon, Washington, and California, the berries can ripen from mid-June to late July. They grow well in the deep woods, as in alder thickets and stream bottoms.

They were an important food for indigenous peoples, often mixed with fish or fat. They are not practical to dry because of their water content, but they make good grazing because they pick easily and the plants are more user-friendly than blackberries.

A relative of the raspberry, the salmonberry is highly edible but less flavorful. Photos: Wikipedia.

WILD RASPBERRIES
A Wild Woods Treat

Two species of wild black raspberries, *Rubus occidentalis* (eastern) and *Rubus leucodermis* (western), are native to North America. Cultivars of the western variety are grown in Oregon and are usually called black caps.

The wild black raspberry is also closely related to the red raspberries of commerce, sharing the distinctively white underside of the leaves and fruit that readily falls when ripe, although it has more and better stickers. These berries are so delicious, you will not notice the stickers.

Wild black raspberries usually grow 4–8 feet tall, depending on setting, soil, and water. The fruit usually matures in early summer, depending on the year. As bird-seeded volunteers or feral domestic varieties, raspberries may be found in all temperate zones.

Black wild raspberries just may make the best jelly in the world. They tend to be a little sweeter than red raspberries, a close relative. Photo: Wikipedia.

WILD BLACKBERRIES
Think Pie on the Run

Few fruits can compete with blackberries as desirable food in the wild. There are hundreds of varieties native to the Americas, yet one of the most common in the western U.S. woods is the feral "Himalayan" cultivar. Thornless cultivars have been developed. They are in the rose family, related to others such as raspberries.

The only warning necessary regarding wild blackberries is beware of competing wildlife. About the time blackberries come on, black bears are starting to fatten up, and they may not want to share, and mamma may have young with her. For trivia freaks, note that blackberries are not berries; they are an aggregate fruit, and blackberry thorns are not really thorns, they are prickles. Tell *that* to Br'er Rabbit! Note that the very early spring shoots of blackberry, raspberry, salmonberry, and thimbleberry when still very tender are edible. Blackberry root is regarded as edible when peeled; the whole root has long been used as a folk remedy in England for diarrhea.

The kid's riddle always was, "What's red when it's green?" Blackberries have a longer season than some fruit because it does not all ripen at once. Photo: Wikipedia.

HUCKLEBERRIES AND BLUEBERRIES
Yes, There Is a Difference

Not that you'd care in the wild, but although they are related, there is a difference in blueberries and huckleberries. Some blueberries are red, and some huckleberries are blue, and they grow and taste very much the same. The difference is that a huckleberry has 10 hard seeds, whereas a blueberry has numerous soft seeds. A huckleberry's stem is smooth; a blueberry's stem is bumpy and "warty." The foliage of huckleberry plants feels stickery compared to that of the blueberry. There are many cultivars of blueberry, not so of huckleberries. Aficionados (i.e., people who harvest them wild) maintain huckleberries have a superior taste. I'm inclined to agree, especially in comparison to the watery farm-raised blueberries you find in the market.

In the wild, however, they are all a superior and healthy fruit except for a weird little pink variety that grows almost solitary in the deep woods . . . as long as you do not mind a little competition from bears. There are innumerable varieties of each.

Typical blueberries and (left) typical huckleberry on Mt. Hood, Oregon. Photos: Wikipedia.

STRAWBERRIES
You Already Know These . . .

Native wild and animal-seeded strawberries will be found in all temperate zones. Get a feel for the saw-toothed leaves and you won't pass these by. Ones growing in the woods (pictured) usually have an upright stem, are usually solitary, and have smaller and very soft fruit. Ones common to meadows are firmer and superior eating, and often are in small patches. The leaves make a good tea. Photo: Wikipedia.

THIMBLEBERRY
A "Where's the Beef?" Berry

Thimbleberries are native to the northern and western United States and are usually found at the edge of woods and along railroad tracks and logging roads. A relative of the raspberry, the thimbleberry is less flavorful and not very substantial, but the berries fall easily from the bush when ripe and there are no real stickers to deal with. The large, softly fuzzy leaves are handy for hygiene in the woods. Photo: Wikipedia.

PAWPAW
King of the American Wild Fruits

This fruit is a real treat for those grazing down east in the fall. Pawpaw is the largest edible native fruit in North America and one of the most delectable. It is not grown for market, as it only keeps a day or two off the tree and does not ship well at all.

Asimina triloba is native to the eastern, southern, and midwestern United States and southern Ontario, from New York west to eastern Nebraska, and south to northern Florida and eastern Texas. The

Were it not for its range all the way into Canada, the pawpaw might be mistaken for a tropical fruit. Photo: Wikipedia.

pawpaw is a shrubby tree with smooth bark that grows to 35 feet, and its leaves turn bright rusty-yellow in the fall, making the usually clonal groves easy to spot. The leaves are about 10 inches long and 4–5 inches across.

The fruit of the pawpaw is a large, yellowish-green to brown berry, 2–6 inches long and 1–3 inches in diameter, often weighing more than a pound. The fruit contains large brown seeds embedded in the soft, sweet fruit pulp. The conspicuous fruits begin developing after the plants flower. They are initially green, maturing by September or October to yellow or brown. Most people say they taste a lot like bananas but juicier. I think they are better than bananas. If not for their limited range, they would be king of American wild fruits.

BRACKEN FERN
How Hungry Are You?

No book on grazing the local real estate would be complete without talking about bracken fern. Coverage will be somewhat different, however, than the cavalier regurgitations one usually reads of how the natives worldwide have made use of it, and how tasty it is, and how you aren't cognoscenti if you don't eat bracken fern.

With several subspecies, bracken does grow worldwide, and people from Europe to New Zealand and in between have eaten it. That's the good news. The bad news is, just because your ears don't fall off when you eat some doesn't mean it isn't poisonous. It is carcinogenic to people and to animals such as mice, rats, horses, and cattle when eaten. Most animals will avoid it unless nothing else is available, although every spring our goats ate it and the milk tasted like asparagus. In spite of positively being identified as a carcinogen, the young fiddleheads are still commonly eaten in China, Japan, and Korea, where some researchers suspect a link between consumption and higher stomach cancer rates. Even the spores have been implicated as a carcinogen. Danish scientist Lars Holm Rasmussen released a study in 2004 showing that the carcinogenic compound in bracken, ptaquiloside or PTQ, can leach from the plant into the water supply, which may link to an increase in the incidence of gastric and esophageal cancers in bracken-rich areas, whether it is being eaten or not.

In cattle, acute bracken poisoning can occur if they eat it, and in pigs and horses bracken poisoning induces vitamin B deficiency, where it damages blood cells and destroys thiamine, and causes beriberi. The major toxin in bracken is ptaquiloside. The carcinogenicity of ptaquiloside was proven in 1984, and ptaquiloside was

Delicious and in many ways nutritious, bracken is also toxic and a carcinogen. Beware the advice of those who recommend it. Photo: Wikipedia.

shown to be responsible for the immediate characteristic biological effects of bracken, such as acute bracken poisoning, bright blindness in sheep, mutagenicity, clastogenic effects, and genotoxicity.

So, the question here becomes, just how hungry are you? Once the bitter brown fuzz is washed off young fiddleheads, they can be used as, and taste very much like, asparagus. New Zealand natives dried the roots as trail food and would pound them and suck out the starch as needed. Worldwide, everybody has a favorite recipe. But if a pig won't eat it unless he's starving, and when he does eat it he gets beriberi, I ask again, in light of recent research, *just how hungry are you?*

CAMAS
Look for the Blue Flower

There are half a dozen species in the *camassia* genus that are native to western North America, with a native range from British Columbia to northern California and east to Wyoming, Montana, and Utah. Many towns, places, and even railroads have been named for the camas, aka, camass or quamash. There is a similar variety native to the East, often called "wild hyacinth."

Camas can grow prolifically in moist meadows. They are perennials and have basal linear leaves measuring 8 to 32 inches long, which emerge in early spring. The flower stalks can be from 1 to 4 feet high, with one to several flowers on the stalk in summer. The flowers are critically important because they are the best identifier between true camas (highly edible) and "death camas" (which is not a true camas and is highly toxic). Both the true camas and the so-called death camas flowers have six petals*, but true camas flowers will be pink, pale lilac, blue, or purple. Death camas flowers are white (flower blue = good for you). White-flowered death camas can grow in the same field: beware! The bulbs look similar—go by the color of the flower.*

Spreading from seed, unmolested camas can take over whole meadows and are a beautiful sight—especially if you are hungry. *Camassia* species were an important food staple for Native Americans and settlers in parts of the Old West and were a survival staple on the Lewis and Clark Expedition of 1804–1806.

The onion-shaped bulbs are best harvested in the autumn but are good any time you can positively identify them. Native Americans pit-roasted or boiled them. They taste like a very sweet sweet potato,

Edible camas will have blue-to-purple flower. White-flowered look-alikes are poisonous. Photo: Wikipedia.

with a slightly coarser yet gooey texture. At home, I like 'em buttered and baked in foil. They contain inulin, like Jerusalem artichokes, but have a richer flavor. They can be dried hard and pounded into a sweet flour.

The camas does well in gardens and has a pretty flower, much like a hyacinth. Preferring rich, well-drained soil, it adapts to lightly shaded woods on rocky outcrops, as well as in open meadows, and makes a fun option for those who like to graze their flower garden, or like no-maintenance landscaping they can harvest. You can divide the bulbs in late fall, if you want to. But it is easier to plant seeds.

Properly identified, camas is one of the truly premium field foods.

WAPATO (ARROWHEAD)
Many Varieties and Venues

Sagittaria, in different varieties all over the world known as arrowhead, is native to much of North America, including most of Canada and the western and northeastern United States, and is commonly called wapato. A flowering aquatic plant in the water plantain family, most common in North America is *Sagittaria cuneata*, shown here. It is variable in appearance across individuals and varieties, and submerged parts of the plant look different from those growing above the surface or on land—but a common denominator is the commonly arrowhead-shaped leaf. In general it is a perennial herb growing from a white or blue-tinged tuber. It has a white male or female flower.

The entire rhizome is edible, even raw, and the stems are edible if cooked. Unwashed tubers store well and were a staple of Native Americans. Used like a potato, the tubers are slightly crunchy even when cooked, and they may be boiled, sliced, and dried for later use. In shape, they remind me of a large "button" mushroom growing upside-down.

Underwater tubers usually can be dislodged with your feet and they will float. I've seen native folks in Washington using a clam rake, which works well but is probably hard on the bed. Tubers are more work above the water line, as they often grow several feet from the parent plant, but they are worth the work. In ideal conditions, they grow almost to the exclusion of everything else in the marsh.

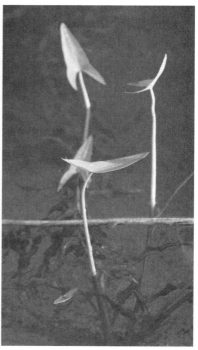

Above: Wapato can vary greatly in size and individual shape but almost always has the characteristic arrowhead leaf. Photo © by Richard Old, www.xidservices.com.

Top right: When competing on land, the wapato tends to grow smaller leaves. Photo © by Richard Old, www.xidservices.com.

Right: Arrowhead is easiest to harvest in shallow mud by dislodging the tubers with your feet or digging sticks. Photo: Wikipedia.

MINER'S LETTUCE
The '49ers' Greens on the Go

This is a good and good-for-you trail food, popular with the '49ers (1849ers, that is) who ate it during the California Gold Rush for its vitamin C to avoid scurvy. It's a fleshy annual plant native to the Western mountain and coastal regions of North America from southern Alaska to Central America. It's common all through the Northwest, but most common in California in the Sacramento and northern San Joaquin valleys.

It's a low-growing plant that favors light shade as found in moist woods. It smells like lettuce when crushed and tastes like lettuce but with a stronger flavor, rather like purslane. Leaves and stems are pulpy and succulent but thinner than purslane. The stem that will bear the flower appears to come up through the middle of one round leaf, which is actually two leaves that grow together.

It's a good graze-and-go food raw or in salads, or it may be boiled. Any recipe for purslane will work well with miner's lettuce.

It is common in the spring, and it prefers cool, damp conditions. It first appears in sunlit areas after the first heavy rains. The best stands are found in shaded areas, especially in the uplands, into the early summer. The small flowers are white or pink, flat, with five petals, and appear from February to June depending on location. Flowers are grouped from a few to many above a pair of leaves that are united together around the stem and look like one circular leaf. Mature plants have numerous erect to spreading stems that branch from the base. As the days get hotter and the leaves mature and then dry, they turn a deep red, like purslane. It's all edible, and a tasty green.

If you like lettuce, you will like miner's lettuce very much. Photo: Wikipedia.

Eating on the Run

SHEEP SORREL (SOURGRASS)
For Refreshing Trail Grazing

As kids, everybody ate "sourgrass." This European transplant is now "native" to all 50 states. In wet areas, it is a succulent and refreshing harbinger of spring. Eating on the run, I would not count on it for a great deal of nourishment—first, because it doesn't contain a lot, and second, because I do not think it would be healthy to eat more than snack or seasoning amounts of it.

Its refreshing tartness comes from its oxalic acid content, like rhubarb. A little is tolerable to most folks, like you would get in rhubarb pie or spinach, but a lot is simply not healthy and contributes to the formation of calcium oxalate-based kidney stones, and according to some studies, regular intake of oxalic acid interferes with calcium uptake. One reference I was enjoying a great deal for its firsthand research on wild foods speculated that strong oxalic acid had no more dietary impact that the acetic acid in vinegar! Don't believe it. Of course, the author of the reference was a bright but young man who had not yet hung onto the doorpost and screamed as he passed his first kidney stone.

But aside from that, sheep sorrel makes a refreshing trail treat and a nice addition to otherwise bland greens, and you're likely to find it anywhere. The specimen shown here is past its prime, and in need of a drink, but you could still grab some nice leaves off the right side of the plant.

Grown (and eaten) all over, sheep sorrel is a tart, refreshing herb taken in moderation. Photo: Wikipedia.

PRICKLY PEAR CACTUS
The Desert Rose Is Good to Eat

I lived for many years in the Sonoran Desert, and although it is generally regarded as mostly just sand and rock, there is food all over the place. And the nice thing about it is, it's generally pretty easy to spot.

There are many varieties of prickly pear (aka, paddle cactus), and they're all good to eat. Photo: Wikipedia.

Prickly pear has a wide venue throughout the temperate regions of the world, and it's tasty. Not particularly friendly but very tasty. The flowers are edible, sweet and delicious. The pads are the staple part of the plant. Use or make some tongs to handle them and roast them lightly over a fire or flame to burn off the stickers and fuzzies (glochids); continue to roast and the skin will usually peel right off, or you can use a knife. You can just spear chunks and roast them as a shish kebob or slice and bread them with egg like you would eggplant and fry them at home. You can also eat raw, but they have a lacy, fibrous texture inside, especially if they're a little dry, that can be hard to digest raw. They taste a little woody, a little like bitter cucumber raw. When the fruit is in season, roast them also over a fire long enough to burn off the fuzzies, and when the skin splits, peel it off. You'll find lots of large seeds, but most taste very much like huckleberries. The seeds make good flour. Although you wouldn't do this on the move, they make excellent juice and jelly. *If it looks like a prickly pear but has a milky sap, it is not a prickly pear.*

SAGUARO CACTUS
It's Work but Worth It

The fruit of the giant saguaro cactus, usually ripe around June, is not easy to get—but it's worth it. Growing at the ends of arms and atop a mature saguaro, the succulent red fruit will be a couple inches long, about an inch in diameter, and contain thousands of tiny black seeds. When ripe, the fruit splits open lengthwise, and you use a long rib from a dead saguaro to knock them off. They are one of nature's greatest treats, tasting like wild strawberries but better.

At the ends of arms and atop a mature saguaro, the nectar-rich blossoms are pollinated by bats at night and birds during the day. Photo: Wikipedia.

ARIZONA CEREUS CACTUS
The Surprise in the Dirt

I wonder if this may not have been placed in the desert just to remind us that things are better than they seem. The Arizona cereus, *Peniocerus greggii,* is now protected, but before population pressure and loss of habitat, it provided a desert treat to the natives who lived in the Sonoran Desert.

It was more than 40 years ago that I was working with a cat skinner punching through a road when he dismounted and grabbed a shovel. I thought he had spied a snake, but he walked over to a spindly, dead-twig-looking plant in the lee of a palo verde tree that I would have taken from a distance as a dying stag-horn cholla cactus. With tender care he excavated around and around until he had exposed a root the size of a watermelon, with an outside texture and color of a jicama root. He wrapped the whole thing in a tarp and took it home. Early the next summer he called me to come over that night to see one bloom. This cactus blooms once a year, just after dark, for a few hours, and then the flower wastes away and bears an orange fruit. The bloom is worth the wait. It is large and has the intoxicating scent of vanilla beans on steroids. Stunning. Later, after accidentally plowing one through, he brought me some of the cutoff his wife had baked. It was delicious—sweet, starchy, and filling.

You will usually find them growing discreetly under the protection of other growth, like a palo verde or mesquite or cat-claw acacia, and you have to look sharp because they are spindly and only grow to a few feet. They are easy to identify once spotted, because in cross-section the stalks and branches are three- or sometimes four-lobed. Once I began looking for them, they proved not that

If a flower is supposed to be beautiful and smell good, then *Peniocerus greggii* is the best in the business. Photo: University of Arizona Tucson, Boyce Thompson Arboretum.

uncommon in remote areas. One night I was walking back from a broken-down rig, down a sandy wash because I knew where it went, and I found one by its scent, 50 feet away from the wash. Broken down or not, I had to go find it and admire the flower. I think that's before they had invented aromatherapy—but it worked for me! But leave 'em alone unless you are starving.

MESQUITE BEANS
A Tree in the Pea Family

In the pea family, several varieties of mesquite grow in the Southwest, both native and hybrid species. The bean pods of the mesquite are good, and good for you, and usually hang on the tree well past maturity, until a desert critter harvests them. Virtually all desert herbivores and rodents make use of them. I used to pound the seeds free of the pod and make a mush out of the pod, which tastes like pumpkin. The hard seeds can be ground into flour, which adds a nutty flavor to breads and biscuits. Use about a third bean flour with two-thirds glutinous flour so it will hang together. Mesquite powder is high in calcium, magnesium, potassium, iron, and zinc, and is rich in the amino acid lysine. You can even boil the sweetish pods and reduce the water to make jelly or wine.

The spring flowers are like long, floppy, yellow catkins; have a lovely, lemon-rose scent; and are edible—slightly sweet. I've seen deer eating the young, green pods, but to me they taste woody and bitter. The mature, dry pods make a decent trail food, but you're a better man than me if you can eat the hard seeds. Even coyotes eat mesquite beans when times are hard, but you can tell from the scat that they don't chew the seeds either. Mesquite seeds must be pounded with a rock or milled and be well cooked to be safe nutrition. Some sources say mesquite beans should be cooked to destroy an anti-nutrition protein that interferes with enzymes which convert proteins into amino acids, as well as phytohemagglutinins, which are also found in red kidney beans, which is why *raw* kidney beans are toxic and must be boiled. But mesquite beans are so very hard, I can't imagine anyone being able to eat them unless they have been boiled for a long time, even when milled.

Nature's bean patch, and you don't even have to bend over to pick them. Just remember that the seeds must be thoroughly cooked. Photo: University of Arizona, Tucson, Boyce Thompson Arboretum.

PALOVERDE BEANS
The Green Pole Tree

Another staple of native peoples in the Southwest deserts was the seed of the paloverde tree. They were eaten both raw and roasted, or were ground into fine flour and mixed with water and cooked as a soup base. They were also served as a drink. There is more than one variety of paloverde native to the area, and all are easy to identify by their pale green bark: the leaves (see photo) are small and discreet, and drop off during times of drought, but the bark contains chlorophyll required for photosynthesis. In a moist spring, the tree blooms with fragrant yellow flowers.

Paloverde is Spanish for "green pole"—an apt description for this shrubby desert tree that has chlorophyll in its smooth, green bark. The leaves (right) are very small and fall away during drought. Photo: University of Arizona, Tucson, Boyce Thompson Arboretum.

YUCCA
The Original Pokemon
Is Good Food

Various species and subspecies of yucca are ative over most of the United States and up into Canada, and are very common in the warmer, drier areas. Indigenous peoples have made use of their fibrous leaves for textiles and cordage, the roots of some species for medicine and soap, and the flowers, fruits, flower stalks, and seeds as food. Fruits vary from "doable" to tasty; seeds usually don't amount to much. However, the tall flower stalk that quickly shoots up and looks like a giant asparagus on the ones common to the Sonoran Desert, the "soaptree" yucca (*Yucca elata)*, is very sweet with a molasses flavor before the flowers appear. This stalk can be sliced and dried.

There are nearly 50 species of yucca and some two dozen sub-species, and although their size and proportions may vary, they are all obviously related. Fibrous, sharply pointed leaves vary from robust as on this Mojave yucca to thin and flexible on the soaptree (right). Photos: Wikipedia.

CONCLUSION

The body of knowledge regarding man's hard-won successes in his search for edible and healthy vegetation would fill libraries, and that's just the cultivars. There are likely as many or more edible plants that simply do not lend themselves to cultivation, or efficient and profitable marketing. And then there is the rest of the vegetable kingdom, which are either unwholesome, toxic, or outright deadly.

The purpose of this volume has been to give the reader a practical familiarity with the common wholesome, edible plants that are likely to be found in the North American wild. The edible plants chosen for inclusion here are those that are most widely found, most readily identified, and require the least, if any, preparation—and have a history of use as food.

No attempt has been made to even broadly define those plants that are poisonous. Likewise, I have striven to avoid including potentially good plants that are likely to be confused with poisonous plants, because confusion runs both ways. There are plants that can be toxic but can be made edible if properly prepared. We have avoided those as well except for those requiring basic cooking, because the premise has been to feed a person who may need to keep moving. It is my hope that whether you are moving to or are moving from, this work will help keep you fueled until you get there.

I've covered a sampling here that you may have seen but maybe didn't know you could eat and that may pique your interest to give the genre a fair trial. Your and your own palate can take it from here. Get a good color field guide for positive ID, as "unknowns" can be toxic, and then take to the field to harvest and learn before you need to. And remember that although plants listed here have been eaten for centuries, some folks do have individual food allergies.